REIMAGINING ADVOCACY

RSA·STR

THE RSA SERIES IN TRANSDISCIPLINARY RHETORIC

Edited by
Michael Bernard-Donals *(University of Wisconsin)* and
Leah Ceccarelli *(University of Washington)*

Editorial Board:
Diane Davis, *The University of Texas at Austin*
Cara Finnegan, *University of Illinois at Urbana-Champaign*
Debra Hawhee, *The Pennsylvania State University*
John Lynch, *University of Cincinnati*
Steven Mailloux, *Loyola Marymount University*
Kendall Phillips, *Syracuse University*
Thomas Rickert, *Purdue University*

The RSA Series in Transdisciplinary Rhetoric is a collaboration with the Rhetoric Society of America to publish innovative and rigorously argued scholarship on the tremendous disciplinary breadth of rhetoric. Books in the series take a variety of approaches, including theoretical, historical, interpretive, critical, or ethnographic, and examine rhetorical action in a way that appeals, first, to scholars in communication studies and English or writing, and, second, to at least one other discipline or subject area.

Other titles in this series:
Nathan Stormer, *Sign of Pathology: U.S. Medical Rhetoric on Abortion, 1800s–1960s*

Mark Longaker, *Rhetorical Style and Bourgeois Virtue: Capitalism and Civil Society in the British Enlightenment*

Robin E. Jensen, *Infertility: A Rhetorical History*

Steven Mailloux, *Rhetoric's Pragmatism: Essays in Rhetorical Hermeneutics*

M. Elizabeth Weiser, *Museum Rhetoric: Building Civic Identity in National Spaces*

Chris Mays, Nathaniel A. Rivers, and Kellie Sharp-Hoskins, eds., *Kenneth Burke + the Posthuman*

Amy Koerber, *From Hysteria to Hormones: A Rhetorical History*

Elizabeth C. Britt

REIMAGINING ADVOCACY

Rhetorical Education in the Legal Clinic

THE PENNSYLVANIA STATE UNIVERSITY PRESS
UNIVERSITY PARK, PENNSYLVANIA

Library of Congress Cataloging-in-Publication Data

Names: Britt, Elizabeth C. (Elizabeth Carol), 1964– author.
Title: Reimagining advocacy : rhetorical education in the legal
    clinic / Elizabeth C. Britt.
Other titles: RSA series in transdisciplinary rhetoric.
Description: University Park, Pennsylvania : The Pennsylvania
    State University Press, [2018] | Series: The RSA series in
    transdisciplinary rhetoric | Includes bibliographical
    references and index.
Summary: "Investigates how students in a clinical legal
    education program learned to advocate effectively and
    ethically with clients abused by intimate partners.
    Demonstrates the importance of valuing clients as experts
    in their own lives and as equal partners in decision
    making"—Provided by publisher.
Identifiers: LCCN 2017054037| ISBN 9780271081021
    (cloth : alk. paper) | ISBN 9780271081038 (pbk. : alk. paper)
Subjects: LCSH: Abused women—Counseling of. | Social
    advocacy—Study and teaching. | Law—Study and teaching.
Classification: LCC HV1444.B75 2018 | DDC 362.82/
    9286—dc23
LC record available at https://lccn.loc.gov/2017054037

The Pennsylvania State University Press is a member of the
Association of University Presses.

It is the policy of The Pennsylvania State University Press to
use acid-free paper. Publications on uncoated stock satisfy the
minimum requirements of American National Standard for
Information Sciences—Permanence of Paper for Printed
Library Material, ANSI z39.48-1992.

For the clients of the Domestic Violence Institute at
Northeastern University School of Law. You taught
students about advocacy, and they taught me.

Contents

Preface

Although this is a scholarly project, its focus on advocacy for those abused by intimate partners has personal resonance for me. The first detailed account of abuse I heard came from a close family member. I knew that she'd been in a turbulent marriage in the 1970s but had not heard the specifics until I began the research for this book. She was married to a man with high status in their small town who forbade her to make phone calls without his permission, did not allow her to work, gave her an allowance and closely monitored her spending, and required her to be home by five in the afternoon. The first act of violence came three weeks into their marriage, when he shoved her into a wall. Over the next six years and through the arrival of two children, she was belittled, controlled, and beaten. He threatened to kill her and take the children if she left. When she eventually presented her husband with divorce papers, he assaulted her, badly cutting her lip and chin. For some time afterward, her father, ashamed that his daughter's marriage to a prominent member of the community was ending, would not look her in the eye.

Other women I know—family members, friends, and colleagues—have since told me their own stories of abuse. They have shared how they survived isolation, degradation, and severe violence with long-term emotional and physical effects, often with little support. Some of the incidents they recounted were decades old, others fresh. In some cases, just hearing the details left me nauseated and dizzy.

I realized that I was hearing more of these accounts—and more details—because of my research. Although I had previously imagined myself as supportive of women's experiences, I had unwittingly missed opportunities to show that support. I knew the statistics. I knew that domestic violence was still maddeningly pervasive in the US. But like the advocates I follow in this book, I had to learn what to ask and how to listen.

Acknowledgments

This project germinated more than a decade ago, when I attended a conference sponsored by the Domestic Violence Institute (DVI) at Northeastern University School of Law. I attended to learn more about domestic violence and the work of the institute, not knowing that I would eventually want to write a book about them. My deepest gratitude is to the DVI, especially Lois Kanter, founder of the programs described in this book and then executive director of the institute, for allowing me access, providing her own perspectives on my analyses, and offering me opportunities to share the work in her circles. Katherine Schulte, a supervising attorney in the programs when I conducted my fieldwork, provided a careful review of the entire manuscript. I also thank supervising attorney Zoe Paolantonio and administrative assistant Susan Verity at the DVI for their substantive and logistical support, as well as law faculty Margaret Burnham and Jim Rowan for the opportunity to speak to the broader law school community. Thanks finally to current DVI faculty Jennifer Howard and Margo Lindauer for getting me up to date on the programs' evolution.

The book would not have been possible without the law students who generously participated in the study. Although they must remain nameless, they are the heart of the book, and I am profoundly grateful for their willingness to share their experiences with me. Thanks especially to those who offered feedback on the manuscript even after they had graduated and begun their legal careers.

A number of undergraduate students at Northeastern University helped me transcribe interviews. I thank Ali Al-Abdulla, Tim DeJesus, Meaghan Fox, Amanda King, Carolina Marion, Jessica O'Neill, and especially Kimika Ross for their work. Elizabeth Folan contributed original insights in an independent study in which she helped me code interview data. I thank current and former graduate students Charlie Lesh, Stephanie Loomis Pappas, and Eric Sepenoski for invigorating conversations about ethnographic methods, and Erin Frymire, Rachel Lewis, Laura Proszak, and James Stanfill for helping me refine my thinking about legal rhetoric, feminist methodologies, rhetorical education, and rhetorics of the body.

I am extremely fortunate to have had supportive writing partnerships throughout this project. The book has been indelibly shaped by Chris Gallagher and Terese Guinsatao Monberg, each of whom has given me regular, prolific, and insightful feedback from the earliest drafts. I thank them for their brilliance, their honesty, their friendship, their generosity, and their endurance. I thank my writing group from the 2009 RSA Career Retreat for Associate Professors—Janice Chernekoff, Cindy Haller, and Christine Tulley—for more than four years of productive collaboration. Jen Bacon helped me develop what is now chapter 2. Elizabeth Shea talked me through several chapters and gave extensive feedback on the introduction. Marina Leslie has been an accountability partner as well as a steady sounding board and strategist.

The peer review process at the Pennsylvania State University Press has substantially improved the project. I am enormously grateful to Suzanne Enck, along with an anonymous reviewer, for detailed commentary and suggestions on the initial submission. Series editors Michael Bernard-Donals and Leah Ceccarelli, editor in chief Kendra Boileau, and an anonymous member of the board offered additional direction and advice. Thanks also to the entire editorial team for their professionalism in turning my manuscript into a book.

From friends and colleagues around the country, I have received support in the form of helpful conversations, mentoring, letters of support, and editorial feedback. Thanks to Hugh Baxter, Greg Clark, Kathy Colman, Kirsten Davis, Maureen Gallagher, Cheryl Geisler, Michael Halloran, Debbie Hawhee, Jim Jasinski, John Lucaites, James Martel, Raymie McKerrow, Carolyn Miller, Jay Mootz, Roxanne Mountford, Amy Propen, Kris Ratcliffe, Austin Sarat, Mary Schuster, Patricia Sullivan, Jim Turner, and Jim Zappen. A special thanks to Jenny Andrus for collaborating with me, invigorating my thinking, and being a source of inspiration.

My research for this book was supported by a sabbatical leave from Northeastern University in fall 2010. At Northeastern, I am lucky to have had support and encouragement from many colleagues, including Liz Bucar, Victoria Cain, Ryan Cordell, Ellen Cushman, Theo Davis, Elizabeth Dillon, Laura Green, Carla Kaplan, Erika Koss, Lori Lefkovitz, Jack McDevitt, Neal Lerner, Stuart Peterfreund, Mya Poe, Uta Poiger, Nan Regina, and Belinda Walzer.

Dear friends not already named have sustained me throughout the project. Special thanks to Abbie Baynes, Terry Durkin, Gayle Garlick, Deanne Harper, Kathleen Kelly, John Monberg, Julie Wakstein, and Susan Wall for encouraging me in my work and helping me keep it in perspective. My family has listened for years as I've talked through this project in its various incarnations. For their interest and unwavering support, I thank my mother, Carolyn Hammond; my father and stepmother, Earl Britt and Judy Britt; and my brothers and sisters-in-law, Cliff Britt, Mark Britt, Joanna Britt, and Helen Wolstenholme. Benjamin Britt, Josie Britt, Sam Wolstenholme-Britt, and Xan Wolstenholme-Britt have challenged me with their insightful questions about the project and have given me welcome distractions.

To Monkey and Baxter, my feline research assistants, thanks for modeling a healthy work/play balance. And finally to Jeff Strobel, my husband, thanks for being my editor, my friend, my adventure companion, and my partner in life.

Introduction | Bodies, Perspectives, Advocacies

In August 2013, Jennifer Martel of Waltham, Massachusetts, was murdered by her boyfriend, Jared Remy. The son of a well-known broadcaster for the Boston Red Sox, Remy had a long criminal history of domestic violence, threats, and intimidation but had never served time. Two days before the murder, Remy had grabbed Martel by the neck and slammed her head into a bathroom mirror. He was arrested, and Martel obtained a twenty-four-hour emergency restraining order. At Remy's arraignment the following morning, the assistant district attorney recommended—largely because Martel had not sought an extension of the restraining order—that Remy be released without bail. The judge agreed, with a special condition that Remy not abuse Martel. The next day, she was dead, stabbed to death by Remy at their home.[1]

What might have made a difference for Jennifer Martel? According to an independent review, the assistant district attorney should have sought a hearing to determine if Remy was too dangerous to release. The review found that the assistant district attorney had enough information about the seriousness of the assault, Remy's increasingly controlling behavior, and his criminal history to request that he be held without bail until trial or that additional conditions be attached to his release. The assistant district attorney had also misinterpreted Martel's decision not to pursue an extended restraining order as an indicator that she was not at risk. No one from the district attorney's office had talked with Martel about whether she felt safe or connected her with a domestic violence advocate or other resources.[2]

We don't know if Jared Remy would have obeyed an extended order. Research suggests that while restraining orders are largely effective in reducing violence, they are often defied and may precipitate violence.[3] For this reason, many domestic violence advocates consider restraining orders an option that might not make sense in every circumstance. A domestic violence advocate might have asked Jennifer Martel, among other things, a series of questions designed to predict the likelihood that Remy would kill her. The advocate would have learned that Remy had grabbed her by the neck during the assault and that he was very controlling, both strong indicators of homicide risk.[4] The advocate would have asked how Martel thought Remy would react to an extended restraining order and would have helped her strategize about legal and nonlegal options for staying safe. The advocate also could have helped others understand Martel's choices and weigh them appropriately when making their own decisions. If the assistant district attorney and judge had more fully understood this bigger picture, they might have evaluated Remy for dangerousness rather than placing all responsibility with Martel.

In my description of how an advocate might have worked with Jennifer Martel, advocacy is a partnership in which the advocate listens to the client as an expert in her own life and provides access to resources and perspectives that can help the client make decisions. The assumptions underpinning this approach are a far cry from those informing a widely accepted narrative about the role of advocates. (For victims of domestic violence, advocates might include lawyers, staff of district attorneys' offices, volunteers, and others.) According to this widely accepted narrative, an advocate possesses a privileged window into a client's best interests, usually by virtue of professional expertise. Because of this expertise, the advocate's role is to speak and make decisions for the client. In cases of domestic violence, this narrative is further complicated by stereotypes of victims as passive and weak, an attitude expressed in a local newspaper editorial a week after Martel's murder that proclaimed victims of domestic violence "are often the ones least able to think, speak and act in their own best interests."[5]

Advocates operating according to this narrative are motivated by what I call a heroic attitude. Heroic advocates may not recognize that the client has a different but equally important expertise: an expertise in her own life. The heroic advocate may not recognize that the client, inhabiting a different body and having had different experiences, knows things that the advocate simply cannot know. Although perhaps driven by a sincere desire to help, the heroic advocate may undervalue the client's knowledge and ability to act in her own best interest.

My portrait of the heroic advocate is admittedly simplistic. Yet elements of this attitude emerge in empirical studies of lawyers who represent disadvantaged clients. While lawyers for organizations or financially successful individuals tend to take direction from their clients, legal services lawyers—those who help the

- lawyer never described
   in Zora — Sophie doesn't
      like ?.

poor negotiate housing, public benefits, immigration, the criminal justice system, or other issues—tend to take charge.[6] In one study, most legal services lawyers cited their clients' lack of sophistication as a primary reason for assuming a dominant role in decision-making.[7] Recognizing that such lawyer-client roles can exacerbate the problems they are trying to solve, legal scholars specializing in poverty law have developed new models of advocacy for those disadvantaged by the legal system.[8] Legal scholars specializing in domestic violence have had similar insights, recognizing that advocacy strategies too often rely on dominant conceptions of their clients as helpless and weak—and therefore as incapable of making competent decisions.[9]

This book analyzes an effort to teach one of these models to future lawyers. I study two clinical legal programs organized by the Domestic Violence Institute (DVI) at Northeastern University School of Law. In legal clinics, students work with clients, often from marginalized populations, on actual problems. In one of the DVI programs, law students learned to listen to women in the emergency department of a major urban hospital talk about domestic violence. In the other, students learned to help people file for restraining orders in municipal courts. The advocacy model taught in both programs, called *client empowerment*, positions the client rather than the advocate as the primary decision-maker. In the client-empowerment model, the advocate's role is to help the client see available options—legal and nonlegal—and support her in carrying out her own decisions.

As a rhetorician, I am interested in these programs as rhetorical education in advocacy for another. The book analyzes a wide range of rhetorical practices, including speaking, writing, reading, listening, using silence, supporting the rhetorical practices of others, and moving one's body. By calling these practices *rhetorical*, I mean to emphasize that they present a point of view, help constitute identities, and influence thought and action. Central to my analysis is that rhetoric is what Jacqueline Jones Royster calls a "whole-body experience," or action that simultaneously involves thinking, sensing, and feeling.[10]

I use the term *rhetorical education* to refer to the teaching and learning of rhetorical practices as well as the necessarily embodied development of attitudes toward—and capacities for—rhetorical action. Ideally, rhetorical education has a civic function, developing what William Keith and Roxanne Mountford describe as "citizen participants, not simply future employees or more literate students."[11] Through rhetorical education, students ideally develop the capacity to form judgments about issues of public concern and influence others.[12] Because rhetorical education focuses on public life, it has the potential to act with other forms of education to promote social change, even if it cannot solve all social problems.[13] But since rhetorical education is always about power relations—about who can participate and in what forms—it can simultaneously promote the dominant culture while erasing the voices of those from subordinated groups.[14]

I argue in this book that the law students in the DVI programs learned an embodied approach to advocacy that resulted from an expanded notion of expertise based on lived experience. Through rhetorical listening, the students came to understand that because they and their clients inhabited different bodies, they necessarily had different world views and goals and would experience the consequences of any act of advocacy differently. They developed what I call an attitude of deference, which entailed recognizing their clients as experts in their own lives and therefore as having the right and ability to make decisions for themselves. But rather than leaving clients completely to their own devices, students learned practices that supported their clients' rhetorical work, often by drawing on their own knowledge of the law or patterns of abusers. Although these practices did not usually involve speaking for their clients, they constituted advocacy in the sense that they supported their clients' interests. Moreover, advocacy in these settings wasn't performed by any one person occupying a particular institutional role but was distributed across a number of actors, including the client herself. For this reason, I often refer to *advocacies* in the plural. Students learned these attitudes and practices through a range of embodied pedagogies.

This book offers new perspectives to a wide range of readers. To readers in any field, the book provides insight into the value of listening to those abused by intimate partners. Given that a third of women in the US will experience domestic violence in their lifetimes, everyone knows someone it has touched.[15] But many stories remain untold or unheard. Over the years that I have worked on this project, family members, friends, and colleagues have told me about their own experiences, some decades old and some recent. Their stories have shown me the complexity of domestic violence and the challenges victims continue to face, even in twenty-first-century America.

The DVI, as depicted in this book, should inspire those who serve victims of domestic violence. Advocates working on behalf of other populations may also recognize the attitudes explored here and consider ways to improve their own practices or complicate the analyses I have offered. Educators in all disciplines may find ways to adopt or adapt the pedagogies described.

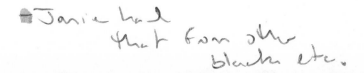
Janie had that from other blacks etc.

This book should spark conversations to connect contemporary American legal education with rhetorical education. Although they were born together in the ancient law courts of Greece and Rome, law and rhetoric are largely separate in the modern research university. For rhetoricians, the book introduces how legal scholars, law teachers, and lawyers theorize, practice, and teach advocacy, a central but largely taken-for-granted concept in our own field. Rhetoricians have much to learn from clinical legal educators in particular, who have developed especially rich ways to account for advocating with others, the central concern of this book. For legal scholars and educators, the book shows how rhetorical theory offers a helpful counterpoint to the decontextualizing tendencies of the predominant pedagogy in American law schools. Reconnecting with rhetoric has the potential to help law schools produce not just competent interpreters of legal texts but citizen participants with practical wisdom.

Legal Education as Rhetorical Education

In ancient Greece and Rome, rhetorical education emphasized the production of rhetors who could perform effectively in both public and private arenas, including the law courts. Specifically, classical pedagogies focused on developing in students the capacity (in Greek, *dunamis*) to deliberate ethically and speak persuasively.[16] Today, however, contemporary rhetorical education and legal education are divided, each devoted primarily to the production of knowledge in their respective disciplines.[17]

Contemporary legal education in the US focuses students' attention on the production of knowledge through a standard method of instruction known as the case method. In the case method, students read appellate judicial opinions, which form the body of American common law. Students learn to see cases as reservoirs of legal doctrine that they can use to predict how courts might interpret similar legal disputes (actual or potential) involving their clients. Because these doctrines are often implied rather than explicit, law students learn to extrapolate them, a process that has come to be known as "thinking like a lawyer."[18]

The case method was introduced in the late nineteenth century at Harvard Law School. Until that time, students learned law either through apprenticeships with experienced attorneys or through the lecture method prevalent at law schools. Even at Harvard, the lecture method was not seen as particularly intellectual, consisting primarily of faculty reading from legal treatises such as Blackstone's commentaries and testing students' abilities to memorize.[19] The case method was part of broader reforms across Harvard University, inspired by the German research university, aimed at making higher education more intellectual by training students to become producers of scientific knowledge. Although today seen as far removed from clinical legal education (CLE), the case method was understood at the time as analogous to clinical *medical* education, in which students learned about medicine by working with patients to understand how to diagnose and treat illness. Unlike medical students, however, law students were to focus not on human beings but on texts; in the words of legal historian Anthony Chase, "law books were to the law student what the bodies of the sick and wounded were to the medical student."[20]

The case method represented a dramatic epistemological shift, characteristic of the new research university, from "shaping the self" to producing knowledge.[21] The method's emphasis on producing knowledge, which remains central today, has been both praised and critiqued. In a 2007 empirical study of sixteen law schools in the US and Canada, researchers sponsored by the Carnegie Foundation argue that the method rapidly inculcates in students the ability to read, think, and argue like members of the legal profession.[22] And in a separate study of eight law schools published the same year (2007), anthropologist Elizabeth Mertz calls the method "an enormously creative system for processing human conflict."[23] However, the case method is criticized by both Mertz and the Carnegie researchers for distancing students from social and moral concerns. By viewing human action through the lens of legal rules, the case method ignores the complex and often painful contexts that form the bases of legal disputes.[24]

According to the Carnegie researchers, CLE is a particularly promising corrective to the decontextualization of the case method. In a legal clinic, students put their knowledge into practice, developing professional judgment through the "experience of lived responsibility."[25] Working with actual clients, students can see that human conflicts are not just legal problems. By noticing the real-world effects of their own judgments, students learn that legal action entails ethical responsibility.

I see legal clinics as a return to the central concern that animated ancient rhetorical and legal education: the production of rhetors. Specifically, CLE has the potential to produce what rhetoricians Marouf Hasian, Celeste Condit, and John Lucaites (writing about legal professionalism) describe as "wise and prudent individuals, trained to interpret the rhetorical culture of their society with creativity, fairness, and decency."[26] This book uses three central and interrelated concepts—embodied knowledge, attitude, and rhetorical listening—to explain how the DVI programs produced rhetors by helping them develop capacities for rhetorical action. I explain each in the following sections. For the most part, the programs are not described in these terms by those who developed them or took part in them; the terms are instead my way of understanding CLE as rhetorical education.

Embodied Knowledge

This book builds on the fundamental insight of feminist standpoint theorists that a speaker's subject position matters to what that speaker knows and says. In other words, every claim to knowledge is located within social and cultural contexts.[27] This insight challenges what philosopher of science Donna Haraway calls the "god trick of seeing everything from nowhere," performed by discourses of modernity such as positivist science.[28] The god trick is the illusion of finding a position from which everything can be seen and understood objectively, without the biases of a particular subjectivity. Knowledge, according to this world view, is abstract and universal, but Haraway insists instead that it is always situated, partial, and—particularly important for this book—embodied. By saying that a speaker's body matters to knowledge, however, Haraway does not mean to imply that some essential, stable, or natural characteristic of someone's body determines what that person knows. Instead, one's viewpoint is grounded in "a complex, contradictory, structuring, and structured body."[29] In other words, while the body shapes what one knows, other forces—social, cultural, economic, and political—in turn shape the body in complex and often conflicting ways.

In the context of advocacy for others, the recognition that knowledge is embodied has important epistemological, ethical, and political implications. Often in advocacy relationships, the advocate is in a more powerful position than the client. When advocates are lawyers, they are more powerful than their clients in relation to the law; they generally know more about the law, legal processes, and particular legal actors. This legal expertise grants lawyers a dominant stance in cultural narratives about lawyering. Lawyers are assumed to be the primary decision-makers and speakers on matters brought before them. With the insight of feminist standpoint theories, however, the client gains the status of subject—a person capable of knowing and speaking—and not just an object, or something about which something is known or said.

The DVI programs helped students develop embodied intelligence, or what the ancient Greeks called *mētis*. Even though all knowledge is embodied, not all pedagogies equally develop this capacity in students. In a book-length study of *mētis*, historians Marcel Detienne and Jean-Pierre Vernant describe it as "a type of intelligence and of thought, a way of knowing . . . [that] is applied to situations which are transient, shifting, disconcerting and ambiguous, situations which do not lend themselves to precise measurement, exact calculation or rigorous logic."[30] Building on Detienne and Vernant, historian of rhetoric Debra Hawhee focuses on *mētis* as embodied, arguing that it "invokes an idea of intelligence as immanent movement" or "a mingling of quick, responsive impulses."[31] Hawhee shows how students in ancient Greece developed *mētis* in both sophistical rhetorical training and athletic training, which often occurred alongside each other. Key to this training was "repeated, sustained engagement" that produced habits enabling quick and appropriate responses.[32]

The DVI programs helped students develop *mētis* through embodied pedagogies. The programs did not explicitly describe their pedagogies as embodied; in fact, the embodied nature of learning and teaching in legal pedagogy has received only limited attention—for example, in arguments for increased use of hands-on activities (such as role-playing, games, skits, and observations) to reach students who learn better through kinesthetic means.[33] Bodies and embodied actions are more explicitly addressed by scholars in rhetoric who study how humans communicate using a broad range of modalities, including not just alphabetic systems but also visual literacies, aural literacies, and bodily movement.[34]

My analysis of the DVI programs examines the relationship between students' bodies and the sites of learning. As rhetorical theorist S. Michael Halloran argues, these sites are significant in rhetorical education because "simply being together in a place . . . calls upon us to attend together to some object of common interest."[35] Classrooms are, of course, a significant site of learning (as Halloran himself indicates). But teacher scholars in many fields are increasingly recognizing the value of learning outside the classroom as well.[36] As I describe in the next chapter, law schools came early to this kind of experiential learning, with some clinics operating at the turn of the twentieth century. Although classroom-based learning still overwhelmingly dominates law schools, many scholars (such as the Carnegie researchers mentioned previously) have called for more out-of-classroom experiences, including but not limited to clinics. One of the most sustained calls has come from Brook K. Baker, who has developed an "ecological theory of learning" that would make practice-based experiences central (rather than peripheral) to legal education. Baker argues that by being physically embedded in "behavior settings," which include courts, law offices, and legislatures, students learn to respond flexibly to real situations.[37]

In many cases, moving students outside the classroom means encouraging them to *act* in ways they would not have inside the classroom. How they act, and what they learn, depends in part on how they understand the purposes of the actions. Philosopher and educational reformer John Dewey, whose work inspires teacher scholars across disciplines interested in experiential learning, explains the relationship between embodied action and purpose. He contrasts a common kind of classroom instruction, in which young children's bodily movements are constrained so that they might attend to lessons, with how a child learns to fly a kite. As Dewey explains about the latter, the child "has to keep his eye on the kite, and has to note the various pressures of the string on his hand. His senses are avenues of knowledge not because external facts are somehow 'conveyed' to the brain, but because they are *used* in doing something with a purpose."[38] Without a sense of purpose, actions are instead mechanical.

But teaching students in nonclassroom settings does not guarantee that the actions won't be mechanical. As literacy scholars Caroline Clark and Morris Young argue, "Simply moving bodies from one place to another" may not serve much of a pedagogical function if students automatically assume predetermined roles.[39] In their analysis of service-learning encounters at community literacy sites, the most successful learning experiences occurred when students negotiated activities (and therefore their roles) with the children they were tutoring. Students came to understand that their role wasn't just to help the children but also to learn about them. These transformations were made possible by the "lived, bodily experiences of social life" at the site.[40]

At the sites examined in this book, law students were constrained from performing the roles they most associated with advocacy. At the hospital, students could not provide advice, and at the court, students did very little speaking in hearings. In both cases, being constrained from slipping into roles they thought they understood provided an opportunity to imagine a different way of advocating for others.

Attitude

The embodied pedagogies of the DVI helped students develop an attitude of deference to the client's expertise in her own life and her ability to make her own decisions. In this book, I draw on the work of rhetorical theorist and critic Kenneth Burke, who saw attitude as mediating between the physical, embodied world and the world of thought and language. Scholars writing about client empowerment do not explicitly characterize the actions and experiences of advocates or clients as embodied. My use of *attitude* as an analytical lens is intended to bring to the fore the latent assumptions about embodiment in this model.

In common contemporary usage, *attitude* often refers to one's mental stance toward something: a "positive attitude" might be seen as the key to attaining one's heart's desires, or a teenager might be reprimanded for having a "bad attitude." Many synonyms for *attitude*, however—*position, standpoint, posture, stance, inclination*—point toward the word's origins not in mental states but in physical ones. According to the *Oxford English Dictionary*, *attitude* in its original seventeenth-century usage referred to a body's position in painting or statuary and slightly later (in the eighteenth century) to a body's disposition in dance. Only in the nineteenth century did the word begin to refer to cognitive states.[41] Burke uses the term with both connotations.

For Burke, *attitude* is the connection between the physical world (what he calls "nonsymbolic motion") and the world of thought and language (what he calls "symbolic action").[42] According to Burke, humans have no control over nonsymbolic motion, such as the wind and ocean currents or many of their own bodily functions, such as blood circulation or digestion. But humans do have some control over symbolic action, which connotes purpose.[43] To demonstrate the difference, Burke uses the example of someone stumbling by accident over an obstruction, which he calls "mere motion." However, if a person "suddenly *willed* his fall (as a rebuke, for instance, to the negligence of the person who had left the obstruction in the way)," the motion becomes more of an action—that is, something purposeful.[44]

Could an observer tell whether the fall was purely an accident? In a more purposeful fall, perhaps the person would make a more exaggerated facial expression of pain. But even the most astute observer would have trouble determining which elements of the grimace were pure reaction (motion) and which were performed for effect (action). That's because the action depends on motion:

to make a face that exaggerates pain, the person relies on physiology. The boundary between action and motion is mediated by *attitude*. In this example, the attitude of the person falling—shock, fear, anger, reproach—marks "the point of personal mediation" between motion and action.[45]

I call attention to the embodied nature of attitude to highlight the role of training in the advocates' education. In their work at the hospital and the courthouse, students had repeated interactions with other people—patients, nurses, doctors, clients, clerks, attorneys, judges, police officers, and so on. They observed and were supervised by more experienced advocates, who reinforced or corrected the students' actions. Over time, they gradually developed an understanding of appropriate deferential action across a range of circumstances. This understanding was both physiological and symbolic, which Hawhee explains as a conjoining of "bodily repetition" and "'knowledge' of what is 'right.'"[46]

Attitudes matter to advocacy because they influence the advocate's actions. Although attitudes are not themselves acts, they are what Burke calls "incipient" acts—they can either take the place of an act or lead to it (e.g., a sympathetic attitude eventually leading to a sympathetic act).[47] Consider how an advocate with a deferential attitude might have worked with Jennifer Martel. The advocate might have asked Martel whether she thought Jared Remy would obey a restraining order and would have helped her strategize about how to keep herself safe. In this example, an attitude of deference leads to a particular act (asking Martel to draw on her own expertise). At the same time, this attitude is a substitute for other more directive acts, such as recommending a restraining order or telling Martel to leave her home.

However, assuming an attitude of deference does *not* mean abandoning one's own responsibilities, as the district attorney's office apparently did in Martel's case. Defending the decision not to pursue a dangerousness hearing or seek bail or additional conditions of release, the assistant district attorney cited a desire to "'respect the victim's wishes.'"[48] But this understanding of a client-empowering approach is mistaken, as explained by staff of Jane Doe Inc., an advocacy organization for victims of domestic violence and sexual assault, shortly after Martel's murder. Taking an empowerment approach, they write, has been "distorted to suggest that victims dictate all the actions of any agency." Instead, others can do their jobs: "The police officer can make an arrest, the prosecutor can request various legal proceedings and options, a dangerousness hearing or stay away order, and the judge can act accordingly."[49]

To assume this attitude and work effectively to support their clients, client-empowering advocates must understand their clients' circumstances, values, and goals. As the Jane Doe Inc. statement puts it, advocates must "engage victims from a place of understanding each individual."[50] Students in the DVI developed an attitude of deference through rhetorical listening, as I explain next.

Rhetorical Listening

Listening is a central rhetorical strategy of the client-empowerment model of advocacy. In an article about the hospital program, the DVI faculty distinguish listening from what normally occurs in an attorney-client interview. In the usual interviewing context, the interviewer is motivated by a "service agenda" that leads to understanding the client "one-dimensionally through her [legal] problem."[51] DVI faculty seek to teach students to instead have a conversation about the client's perspective, helping students "see the client as a whole person."[52] Their goal in having students listen to many women over many months is to help them understand that not all people affected by abuse are the same, even though they may have had similar experiences. Through reflecting on their conversations with the women, students also consider how their own world views affect what they hear.

To understand this strategy, I draw on the work of scholars in rhetorical studies who explore how listening works to achieve cross-cultural competence. For Royster, listening is a means of recognizing different perspectives and conducting oneself respectfully with others.[53] Compared to speaking and writing, listening is often assumed to be something that people do naturally. To counteract this assumption, Krista Ratcliffe uses the term *rhetorical listening* to emphasize that listening is a rhetorical strategy that needs to be theorized and taught.[54] Ratcliffe also claims a broad domain for rhetorical listening; it isn't just something one does with aural texts but a "stance of openness" assumed "in relation to any person, text, or culture" as well as "in cross-cultural exchanges."[55]

This stance of openness is possible only if one recognizes another as someone worth hearing. But according to the DVI faculty, many law students resist the idea that a client's knowledge and experience can be useful in developing advocacy strategies.[56] For this reason, the DVI's pedagogies aimed at helping students notice what Terese Guinsatao Monberg calls "unrecognized rhetorical capacities and imaginings."[57] Looking beyond what is directly visible, as Monberg recommends, is especially important to produce attorneys who can work with clients with different world views and experiences, especially across divides of race and class.

The DVI programs sought to help students communicate across such divides. Contemporary legal education is widely criticized for not preparing students to work with clients, especially clients different from themselves. Critics blame the paucity of practical opportunities as well as the case method, which tends to flatten social categories of identity.[58] But having students work with clients is not enough. Although clinical experiences allow students to interact with real clients, they are too often informed by the same scientistic aspirations as the rest of modern legal education. As a result, they often promulgate one-size-fits-all legal strategies for legal practice.[59] In contrast, clinical programs that attend to cross-cultural communication, like the DVI, aim to produce lawyers who see clients as individuals and as equal partners in decision-making.[60]

About the Site and the Book

The DVI was founded in 1991 by feminist legal scholar Clare Dalton using settlement money from her gender-discrimination lawsuit against Harvard Law School, which had denied her tenure.[61] Northeastern University School of Law was a fitting site for the institute and its clinical programs. Nationally recognized as a leader in practical training and public-interest law, the school is located in Boston, Massachusetts, which has been home since the late nineteenth century to pioneering advocacy movements addressing domestic violence.[62] In the late 1980s, students at Northeastern, along with a number of other law schools, created and ran their own organizations to serve women abused by intimate partners.[63] By 1992, Northeastern University School of Law was one of thirteen US law schools offering faculty-led clinical courses focusing on this clientele.[64] Dozens of law schools around the country now offer clinics that specialize or offer some instruction in advocacy for those affected by domestic violence.[65]

The DVI's programs were developed by Dalton and clinical faculty, principally Lois Kanter, who led the clinics from 1993 until her retirement in 2013. The DVI has a three-pronged mission: (1) to educate not only students but also professionals in other disciplines in the community about domestic violence, (2) to serve women abused by intimate partners, and (3) to conduct research on domestic violence and the effectiveness of interventions.[66] The DVI first established clinics within a community legal aid office and a shelter for abused women.[67] When I began my research, they had two clinics: one in a hospital emergency department and one in nearby district courts. The court program began in 1992 and the hospital program in 1993. The hospital program as described in this book ended in 2011, after the hospital received funding for an in-house advocacy program.[68] As of this book's publication date, the court clinic was still operating, although in a different form.[69]

The DVI was built on a feminist foundation that sees domestic violence as emerging from "socially-sanctioned male entitlement to power and control over his female partner."[70] Despite gains made through the 1994 Violence Against Women Act as well as a host of state laws, abuse against women in the US remains an alarming social problem. Most victims of domestic violence are women; from 1994 to 2010, women accounted for 85 percent of victims of this type of violence.[71] About a third of the women in the US have experienced domestic violence, and nearly a quarter have been kicked, beaten, strangled, burned, cut, shot, or subjected to other forms of severe violence.[72] Women are also the usual targets of a kind of abuse that sociologist Michael P. Johnson calls "patriarchal terrorism" or "intimate partner terrorism," characterized not just by violence but also by efforts to control all aspects of the woman's life (e.g., work, money, social relationships, etc.).[73]

My use of the term *victim* deserves some attention. For the most part in this book, I attempt to avoid the terms *victim* and *survivor* when discussing the person abused by an intimate partner, referring most often to *those abused by intimate partners*. The terminology of victimization has proven difficult for feminists attempting to describe the experiences and advocate on behalf of women affected by gendered violence. The difficulty arises from what sociologist Jennifer L. Dunn calls the "cultural code of agency," which assumes that individuals make unfettered choices and can thus always be held accountable for their actions.[74] According to the logic of this code, women can freely choose to stay or leave abusive relationships; if they stay, they are deemed responsible for what befalls them. Working within this logic, early advocates (second-wave feminists in the 1970s and 1980s) emphasized women's victimhood, arguing that they were trapped in relationships (by isolation, manipulation, fear, lack of money, social norms, inadequate responses from police and judges, etc.).[75]

However, the construction of women abused by intimate partners as victims meant that they were often pathologized as passive, weak, and helpless, and those who did not exhibit these characteristics were not seen as real victims. An alternative construction, *survivors*, emerged alongside these depictions.[76] This term emphasizes women's strategies for coping and keeping themselves safe, even if they do not leave the abuser. Contemporary advocacy overwhelmingly depicts women as survivors, although these depictions may also have their own problems. As Dunn explains, by underscoring women's agency, survivor terminology "may only shift responsibility and attention back to them as individuals and away from the social structures and forces that they must overcome."[77]

So far, I have deliberately used the term *victim* to call attention to domestic violence as a social problem affecting women. In addition, not all the women represented by the aforementioned statistics *survived* the violence. In chapter 4, in which I discuss how advocates learned to help people with abuse prevention orders, I use the term *victim* because of the legal context. As rhetorical critic Jennifer Andrus explains in her study of legal representations of domestic violence, victim status is necessary in order for the law to take action.[78] To borrow directly from Andrus, in using the term *victim*, I am "not aligning myself with the legal position, and not conceiving of abused women as essentially victims."[79] Elsewhere, like Andrus, I have used the term *victim* rather than *survivor* in order to avoid confusion that would result from switching between terms.

To learn about women's experiences with domestic violence, students in the hospital program interviewed women only. Students in the court program served anyone who came to the court for an abuse protection order, although most of their clients were women. Materials provided to students in both programs aimed to help students see the impact of race, class, gender, sexual orientation, religion, nationality, immigration status, and disability on domestic violence.[80] These materials had three goals. The first was to explain how victims experienced domestic violence differently depending on their intersectional identities. Students learned, for example, that an abuser in a same-gender relationship might threaten to out a victim as gay or that an abuser of a disabled victim might withhold medication or access to caregivers. The second goal was to introduce students to legal and extralegal institutional responses that could alleviate or exacerbate problems associated with domestic violence. For example, students learned about public assistance available to immigrant victims of domestic violence as well as the potential risk of deportation for undocumented immigrants engaging with the legal system. The third goal was to help students understand how their own identities affected their assumptions about their clients or the actions their clients should take.[81]

I investigated the programs using ethnographic methods. I conducted multiple qualitative interviews with students in both programs (in all, forty-four interviews with twenty students) and completed about 130 hours of observation (at the law school, the hospital, and the court). I describe these methods and provide brief biographies of the participants in the appendices. Because of the importance of place in the embodied pedagogies I analyze, the heart of the book is organized around three sites of learning: the law school, the hospital, and the court.

In chapter 1, I draw on feminist standpoint theory to explain why attending to embodied experiences is important when one person advocates for another. I then describe how the dominant approach to legal education largely ignores clients and how CLE has the potential to help students understand their clients' embodied experiences. This chapter examines the client-empowerment model embraced at the DVI, which emphasizes deference to the client's expertise in her own life and her ability to make her own decisions. The chapter explores how the client-empowerment model theorizes the client and lawyer as situated, embodied actors rather than as the universal, generic subjects of traditional legal education.

In chapter 2, I analyze how law students came to see embodied experience as linked to a kind of expertise. The chapter focuses on a conference on domestic violence attended by law students just beginning the DVI's hospital program. I begin by drawing on rhetorical theory to describe the problem of credibility (*ethos*) for women in general and for those abused by intimate partners in particular. I then analyze the documentary film *Defending Our Lives*, which is screened at the beginning of the conference, arguing that the film encourages students to be open to others' experiences by engaging in rhetorical listening. The film tells the stories of women who killed their abusive partners and were subsequently mistreated by the criminal justice system. Finally, I analyze a workshop in which students learned about the tactics of power and control used by abusers, as well as their impact on victims, in order to assess the potential danger posed by abusers. Taken together, viewing the film and participating in the workshop helped students understand the complex realities within which those abused by intimate partners make choices.

Chapter 3 moves outside the law school to examine embodied pedagogies in a program in which law students interviewed female hospital patients about domestic violence. At the conference described in chapter 2, students learned to recognize the expertise of others; in this program, students learned to defer to others through a two-part pedagogy. First, students were constrained from helping in ways that they understood as advocacy. Second, the students learned a mode of interviewing that used rhetorical listening to understand the person's embodied experience, a contrast to traditional forms of legal interviewing. Through this pedagogy, students began to resist the impulse to speak and make decisions for others that dominates traditional legal advocacy.

Chapter 4 moves to a program in which law students learned to help people file for abuse prevention orders in city courts serving a racially, ethnically, and linguistically diverse low-income community. As with the hospital program, the students learned to cultivate an attitude of deference toward clients, but here they learned to put it into embodied action. The chapter first describes how the embodied experiences of the advocates formed the basis for identifications with (and divisions from) their clients and the legal system. The chapter then describes how students learned to perform a set of practices designed to support the rhetorical work of their clients. By performing these practices, students developed an embodied intelligence essential to understanding not only how to perform them but whether and when to do so.

In the conclusion, I offer a theory and pedagogy of embodied advocacies. I close by calling for a conversation about what rhetorical education might look like in both rhetoric and law, reuniting two disciplines that emerged together so long ago.

1

Attitudes toward Advocacy

In September 2013, two weeks after filing for divorce, Jane Aiello of Wilkes-Barre, Pennsylvania, was shot dead by her husband, Vito. She was killed apparently after returning to their home for clothing when she thought he was at work.[1] During their twenty-two-year marriage, Vito had "a history of troubled break-ups" with other women, two of whom had filed for protective orders against him.[2] After one of these breakups, Jane herself had warned police that Vito was on his way to kill his girlfriend. Vito's threat against his girlfriend and his murder of Jane are examples of what Martha R. Mahoney has termed "separation assault," which results when "the batterer's quest for control . . . becomes most acutely violent and potentially lethal."[3] Evidence shows that women who live with an abusive partner are at an increased risk of being killed after leaving the relationship, especially if the perpetrator was very controlling.[4]

Remarks by Jane's divorce attorney suggest that advocates can play an important role for clients in these situations. The attorney said to reporters, "'If I had any inkling this was going to happen, I would have done everything to stop it. I'm devastated and shocked.'"[5] On a news website where the attorney's comments were reported, someone who apparently knew the Aiellos went further, saying directly to the attorney, "He had numerous charges and arrests involving stalking, terrorizing, and threatening to kill others and himself. . . . What part of this did Jane not tell you? Because we know she did [tell you]."[6] This commenter implied that the attorney was at least partly responsible for the outcome, both for professing not to have known the dangers and for not doing something with the knowledge she did have. What exactly this commenter would have had the attorney do or say is unclear. But the comment raises questions about the role of advocates in relation to their clients. What are the implications and responsibilities of advocating on behalf of someone else, someone who inhabits a different body and therefore has had different experiences and will more directly endure the consequences of any advocacy act? Who makes the decisions? Do some kinds of decisions belong to the advocate while others belong to the client? Under what circumstances should the advocate speak for or act on behalf of the client?

This chapter explores these questions to illustrate how the approach to advocacy of the Domestic Violence Institute (DVI) differs from the dominant approach taught in American law schools. One of these differences is a matter of terminology. In legal education and practice, the word *advocacy* has a narrow meaning, usually referring only to oral and written arguments made in formal settings such as trials. Discussions with clients about how to resolve their legal problems are typically called *counseling*. As then DVI director Lois Kanter told me in one of our earliest conversations, the DVI uses the term *advocacy* broadly, more like the community-based organizations that serve those abused by intimate partners. But the difference in terminology also reflects a much deeper divide. These community organizations emerged as part of second-wave feminist activism of the 1970s and 1980s to support women who had been not only abused by husbands and boyfriends but also ignored or mistreated by police, judges, lawyers, social workers, doctors, and others in mainstream institutions. From that early activism came the model of advocacy now dominant in organizations that serve those abused by intimate partners. That model emphasizes client autonomy and empowerment. As sociologist Kenneth Kolb observes in his study of people who work in these organizations, the client-empowerment model is an explicit response to the directive approach taken in mainstream institutions, where professionals tend to tell clients what to do.[7]

The client-empowerment model made its way into legal education by way of clinical education, specifically through programs like the DVI that serve those abused by intimate partners or others on the margins of society, particularly the poor. But *clinical legal education* (CLE) and *client empowerment* are not synonymous. CLE originated in law schools, bringing with it the dominant assumption that attorneys are the primary decision-makers. While not all clinical programs embrace a client-empowerment approach to advocacy, CLE did make an important innovation on which the client-empowerment model could build—namely, the belief that law students should work with actual clients.

The client-empowerment model emphasizes deference to the client's expertise in her own life and her ability to make her own decisions. For advocates embracing the client-empowerment model, developing an attitude of deference depends in the first instance on seeing their clients, themselves, and their relationship with clients as particular rather than generic. These particularities emerge from the unique experiences of the body. A client and an advocate each has a particular body, and these bodies have had experiences that help shape world views both unique to the individual and sharing qualities with others in similar circumstances. When advocates and clients interact, these particularities multiply. As a result, advocacy cannot be reduced to rules that can be generically followed by any advocate with any client in any situation.

In this chapter, I first offer a working definition of *advocacy*. I then examine the tendency in American legal education to teach advocacy separately from clients (or to treat them generically) and how the CLE movement brought the client back into view. Finally, I explore how the client-empowerment model of advocacy pays attention to the embodied particularities of both clients and advocates, which lays the groundwork for an attitude of deference. This attitude is cultivated through the pedagogies described in the remainder of this book.

Advocacy as Embodied Performance of Support

In contemporary public discourse, *advocacy* has two related meanings: (1) to argue for an idea or cause and (2) to represent or speak for someone else.[8] In rhetorical studies, advocacy is a surprisingly taken-for-granted concept, its meanings essentially the same as those circulating in public discourse. Although the word *advocacy* frequently appears in scholarship and textbooks, it is not listed as a key term in encyclopedic overviews of the field (such as Sloane's *Encyclopedia of Rhetoric*, Jasinski's *Sourcebook on Rhetoric*, or Littlejohn and Foss's *Encyclopedia of Communication Theory*) and has been little theorized since Quintilian.[9]

For the purposes of this book, I define *advocacy* as a necessarily relational, partial, and embodied performance of support. This definition builds on the work of anthropologist Kim Fortun, who sees advocacy as "a performance of ethics in anticipation of the future" that isn't always overt or intentional and that may take varied forms.[10] To theorize advocacy as embodied, I draw on Kenneth Burke's recognition that division, the prime instigator of identification, begins at birth.[11] Because people inhabit separate bodies, they have different experiences, a fact that has profound implications for advocacy.

Recognizing the body's importance to advocacy is not new, as indicated by legal practices in the classical period. The term *advocacy* comes from the Latin *advocatus*, the name given in Cicero's time to a friend who provided moral support and encouragement during legal procedures, an "influential [man] who gave weight to the litigant's case by [his] presence on his side."[12] Originally, an *advocatus* did not speak, that role being taken up by the *patronus*, a person gifted with eloquence. Instead, the *advocatus* performed his function through his physical presence alone, providing visual evidence of his friend's *ethos*.[13]

Roman advocacy was a shift from the earlier practices of ancient Athens, where most male litigants were expected to represent themselves.[14] Others could hire a logographer, or speechwriter, to provide advice as well as a complete speech. But the logographer could not perform the speech; the speech had to both come from the mouth of the litigant and also appear as if he had composed it himself. The litigant memorized the text provided by the logographer, thereby "maintaining the fiction that he was speaking extemporaneously."[15] This requirement reflects a sense that subject position matters to knowledge formation and speech, an idea also expressed in sophistic writings such as the anonymous *Dissoi Logoi*, which explores the possibility that one's beliefs are influenced by who one is—where one comes from, one's occupation, and so on.[16] According to this perspective, knowledge is constructed by the knower rather than received from an external source, and each person constructs knowledge based partially on her or his social location.

If social location informs what one knows, then knowledge must be embodied, an idea developed by feminist standpoint theorists, who have paid particular attention to reclaiming vision as an embodied sense. Since Plato, vision has been connected to knowledge through metaphor: we say "I see what you mean" and "The book was illuminating." Paradoxically, however, after Descartes aligned seeing with the soul rather than the body, physical sight has been disconnected from knowledge.[17] The resulting epistemology that permeates positivist science is what Donna Haraway calls "a conquering gaze from nowhere."[18]

If vision is instead seen as "a view from a body," then what one knows is always partial (in the sense of both *incomplete* and *interested*) and situated.[19] One's situated location is simultaneously unique and inextricably linked to the groups of which one is a member. Through membership in groups, which are always defined by structural inequality, individuals develop what Patricia Hill Collins calls a "shared angle of vision."[20] For standpoint theorists, a person located on the margins has a better view of the structural inequalities than someone located in the center. For example, as bell hooks writes about growing up as a black American in a small town in Kentucky, "Living as we did—on the edge—we developed a particular way of seeing reality. We looked both from the outside in and from the inside out. . . .We understood both."[21]

What does this mean for how advocacy can or should be practiced? As a start, advocates would critically evaluate their own perceptions, especially when working across cultural boundaries. When in unfamiliar territory, advocates would recognize that what they think they see may be an illusion informed by their own experiences. Advocates would thus be careful about assuming that they understand a client's situation. This kind of caution is what Jacqueline Jones Royster calls "home training," a code of conduct that demands respect when venturing into other people's "home places."[22] As the term indicates, home training is learned. Although not labeled as such, home training is a primary goal of the DVI, especially its hospital program, in which students learned from women in the community.

If social location affects what one knows, then an advocate's position shapes her knowledge of her client. For this reason, it isn't possible to learn the truth of someone else's experience and then tell the story of that experience in an unmediated way.[23] In the 1980s and 1990s, anthropologists had this insight about the practice of ethnography, leading to new ways of researching and representing the experiences of others.[24] Advocates, like ethnographers, can never act as a neutral conduit through which the experience of another becomes known. Through the act of understanding the other person's story and telling that story to others, the advocate helps create the story itself. In addition, in speaking on behalf of herself or someone else, the advocate is creating her own self.[25] When speaking on behalf of another, these representations influence not only the advocate's story of herself but the client's story as well—that is, the client's story is affected by the *ethos* created by the advocate in the moment of speaking.

What are advocates to do? Some theorists and activists reject the practice of speaking for others, arguing that subordinated people should speak for themselves.[26] Others, such as postcolonial theorist Gayatri Chakravorty Spivak, respond that structures of subordination prevent oppressed people from advocating for their own interests. For this reason, others "must not disown [this job] with a flourish."[27] The task is complicated, however, by the need to avoid seeing the oppressed as embodying authentic experience that needs to be recovered. To avoid essentializing, advocates might "speak *to*" the oppressed, a strategy that Spivak sees as more dialogic than "speaking *for*."[28]

In some situations, those whom philosopher Linda Alcoff calls the "discursively privileged" need to take responsibility for speaking.[29] Choosing not to speak (or to speak only for oneself) is not a neutral choice but a political act with material consequences. But speaking for others should not be done automatically or without careful thought. Those seeking to speak for others should examine the situation through "interrogatory practices" to first determine whether speaking is necessary and then how that speaking should be done. One practice, which will become important in chapter 3, is to fight the impulse to speak. Someone who always wants to speak in all situations, Alcoff says, possesses "a desire for mastery and domination" that must be recognized and resisted.[30]

In legal contexts, lawyers are more discursively privileged than their clients. They know more about the law, legal processes, and legal actors. As the DVI faculty explain, legal education develops in students the misconception that they can solve most client problems through this legal knowledge alone, gained primarily through reading and listening to lectures.[31] Students develop this belief because of the dominance of the case method and coursework that focuses on legal principles. As I discuss next, law schools don't give students much opportunity to interact with clients, think about clients, or imagine possible modes of relating to clients.

Advocacy and Generic Clients in Legal Education

Clients have been largely absent from American legal education since 1920, by which time the case method developed at Harvard had been adopted at nearly every American law school.[32] Focusing on substantive knowledge about legal doctrine, the case method pervades both first-year curricula, which are remarkably uniform across the country, and upper-level electives.[33] According to critics, this curriculum teaches students an "insistently generic vision of the world,"[34] one that treats clients as "walking bundles of legal rights and interests rather than as whole persons."[35]

In the case method, clients exist, if at all, in hypothetical scenarios that guide discussions of how judicial opinions can inform potential real-world scenarios. These discussions create what legal scholar Ann Shalleck calls "cardboard clients," or discursive representations that function primarily to demonstrate legal principles. These cardboard clients are created through two features of case method pedagogy. First, students learn to recite facts of the case as they are represented in court opinions. These versions of the facts are usually treated as reality rather than one interpretation of it. For Shalleck, the recitation of facts in the case method "strips the clients of individual identity, wiping out any of their unique understandings of, or experiences in, the world." Second, students are often asked to imagine how they would argue for the plaintiff or defendant in a given case. In their exchanges with faculty, students are trained to understand clients using categories of legal analysis rather than imagining how these particular clients might experience the world. In most cases, there's also no discussion about whether these strategies should be discussed or negotiated with clients themselves.[36]

Law students engage in these exchanges day in and day out throughout the first year of law school, which many scholars see as transformative to students' ways of thinking.[37] These discussions are habituated, part of the everyday and eventually taken-for-granted reality constructed by the case method, developing what sociologist Pierre Bourdieu calls the "legal habitus," or a set of dispositions that "structure the perception and judgment of ordinary conflicts" into legal categories.[38] For Bourdieu, the habitus is not a mechanistic response to rules or a set of conscious operations but "regulated improvisations" that emerge from embodied practices.[39]

The attitude toward clients developed as part of the legal habitus is thus deeply entrenched and difficult to change. Even with minimal exposure to actual clients or representations of them in legal texts, students form the foundation for how they will eventually engage with clients in practice. As Burke explains, attitude can be "preparation for action" so that the character of the attitude will inform the character of the act.[40] The eventual acts by lawyers who have developed the legal habitus are joint products of the lawyers and the legal system, including its means of training.

In the modern law school curriculum, students have opportunities to work with actual clients (usually in the form of clinical courses, paid summer work, internships, and externships), but these opportunities are not well integrated with their doctrinal courses. From the earliest days of the case method, students have wanted more of these opportunities. At the turn of the twentieth century, students at a number of law schools created "legal dispensaries," or volunteer organizations designed to give practical experience to students and legal advice to clients who could not afford it.[41] At the same time, some writers were calling for law schools to more fully integrate client practice into the law school curriculum. Writing in 1917, one of these commentators argued that the clinical experience engaged students not with "dead letters descriptive of past controversies" but with "living issues" of the day; this involvement was so important, he argued, that clinical education should extend throughout the entire law school curriculum rather than being a peripheral add-on.[42]

Two early critics of the case method wanted law schools to be more like medical schools, where students learned primarily by working with patients. According to a 1921 report by the Carnegie Foundation, legal education was too narrowly theoretical, not attending enough to either practical training or a "general education" that would contribute to better citizenship.[43] Contrasting professional law schools with the "clinical facilities" of medical schools, the report argued that the failure was worst at those law schools that had most fully embraced the case method.[44] A similar comparison was made in a 1933 article often cited as a landmark for the CLE movement. According to this article, too many law professors had never practiced law and were therefore incapable of turning out students who could practice, unlike professors in medical schools, who "diagnosed the ailments of flesh-and-blood human beings."[45]

Despite these efforts, CLE did not become widespread until "the social ferment of the 1960s."[46] In 1969, civil rights attorney and law professor Arthur Kinoy suggested that legal education, as well as the profession as a whole, was undergoing a crisis of relevance in the face of the Vietnam War and race-related civil unrest.[47] Law schools, he maintained, needed to help "law serve the needs of people in struggle"; the clinic should be the core of the law school, organized around faculty and students engaged in "efforts to relate the law and its processes to the agonizing, difficult, and as yet unresolved problems of contemporary American society."[48] These goals were shared by the Ford Foundation, which provided seed money to establish clinics at 107 law schools from 1968 to 1978. By the end of the twentieth century, nearly every American law school had some form of clinical education program.[49]

In the twenty-first century, CLE has become prominent in discussions about legal education reform. These discussions were provoked not only by the 2007 Carnegie report (which recommended substantial changes to legal education aimed at integrating theoretical and practical knowledge) but by the economic downturn of 2008, which saw graduates from even the top schools unable to find law-related employment and pay off staggering student loan debt.[50] The resulting drop in enrollments and "diminished public confidence in the system of legal education" prompted the American Bar Association (ABA) to acknowledge in a 2014 report that more attention needed to be paid to "developing the competencies and professionalism required of people who will deliver [legal] services."[51] Although core curricula remain largely unchanged, all students at ABA-accredited law schools as of 2014–15 must complete an experiential component, such as a clinic or simulation, totaling at least six credit hours.[52]

The explosion of CLE programs in the 1970s brought with it a demand for teaching materials, resulting in the publication of a number of textbooks focused on working with clients.[53] One of them, Binder and Price's *Legal Interviewing and Counseling: A Client-Centered Approach* (1977), introduced what has become the predominant lawyering theory taught in clinical programs and what legal scholar Katherine Kruse says is "one of the most influential doctrines in legal education today."[54] (Despite the similar name, client-centered lawyering is not the same as the client-empowerment approach of the DVI, which I discuss later on.) The most recent version of the textbook describes client-centered lawyering as focusing on clients' nonlegal as well as legal concerns, working with clients to solve problems, and recognizing that clients should make important decisions. Some of the advice recognizes the embodied nature of lawyer-client interactions; lawyers are encouraged to design their offices to put clients at ease, meet clients in the waiting area of their offices, smile, and pay attention to attire (e.g., sports clothing) that might give an opening for small talk. When meeting clients in jails or prisons, lawyers are advised to "give clients whatever bit of privacy and dignity the space permits," including closing doors when possible or facing away from security guards.[55]

Some critics say that client-centered lawyering, on the whole, hasn't disrupted the tendency to view clients as homogeneous. Legal scholar Michelle Jacobs, for example, argues that most client-centered textbooks neglect seeing interactions between lawyers and clients as affected by race, class, or gender. By treating client interviewing and counseling as "race-neutral," she says, client-centered lawyering has tended to "suffer from the same error that plagued the traditional approach to law teaching, [i.e.,] . . . the claim that skills and law can be taught as neutral objective principles."[56] Such concerns have led to increased calls for the integration of critical pedagogies into CLE. A recent sourcebook for clinical instructors by three leading CLE scholars, for example, foregrounds the role that intersectional identities (their own and their clients) play in their clients' lives and lawyer-client interactions.[57]

Critical approaches have emerged under a number of different names, among them rebellious lawyering, democratic lawyering, collaborative lawyering, and progressive lawyering.[58] One of these critical approaches is client empowerment. Next, I describe how this approach was developed outside of legal contexts by feminist activists working on the problem of domestic violence.

Client Empowerment Advocacy in Domestic Violence

In 2001, about a decade into the life of the DVI, its faculty published a law review article defining the notion of client-empowerment advocacy in the domestic violence context as "the commitment to and the skill of enabling a client fully to assess her own situation, review the options that are available to her and their implications, and make and carry out those decisions that she believes will most benefit herself and her children."[59] Although domestic violence was recognized as a social problem as early as 1640 in colonial Massachusetts,[60] the notion that those who suffered from it should be empowered to find their own solutions did not emerge in America until the second-wave feminist movement of the 1960s. Along with abortion and rape, woman battering became a central issue for radical feminist activism, fueled by the disclosures of women in consciousness-raising groups about their private experiences.[61] An early feminist-informed shelter for abused women, founded in 1974 in St. Paul, Minnesota, explained that its purpose was "to help such women gain confidence in themselves and acquire power over their lives by fully grasping their possibilities and being supported in their choices."[62]

These early organizations—which often combined shelters with support for finding a job, applying for benefits, or taking legal action—were defined by an *ethos* of self-help informed by feminist critiques of structural inequality. Within a decade, many had been transformed into social service agencies that relied on government funding and professional social workers.[63] The resulting bureaucratization became an ideological issue in the battered women's movement, in part over disparities in how the women were imagined and represented. To attract funding, service organizations needed to represent the women they served as victims with individual problems in need of therapeutic intervention rather than as actors within larger social structures.[64]

While this tension still lingers today, the term *empowerment* is embraced broadly by organizations serving those abused by intimate partners. Jane Doe Inc., a coalition of organizations in Massachusetts that works to prevent sexual assault and domestic violence, lists on its website "empowerment and self-determination" as a core value. It defines *empowerment* as "the right to have control over one's body, mind, and spirit."[65] A similarly expansive approach to empowerment was found by Kolb in his ethnographic study of an agency serving those who had experienced domestic violence and sexual assault. Collectively, the agency called empowerment "inherently respectful of each individual's unique experience and abilities" and "the most effective tool for creating hope and change."[66] Individually, staff members "defined empowerment with broad strokes, leaving the minor details to be worked out on a case-by-case basis."[67] Most often, they defined the term in contrast to the actions of abusers. For these comparisons, they drew on descriptions from a visual tool, widely used by advocates and educators, known as the Power and Control Wheel (see figure 1).

1 | Power and Control Wheel. *Source:* Domestic Abuse Intervention Programs, http://www.theduluthmodel.org.

The Power and Control Wheel was developed in the mid-1980s as part of the Domestic Abuse Intervention Project in Duluth, Minnesota, using descriptions provided by two hundred women in focus-group sessions.[68] It is used today to illustrate the broad range of behaviors that constitute abuse and to argue that these behaviors emerge from a desire to control the victim. For example, the wheel demonstrates the range of behaviors that Jared Remy used to control Jennifer Martel as well as previous girlfriends. The night that Martel obtained her emergency restraining order, Remy had apparently become angry because she wanted to spend time with a friend watching television.[69] On the Power and Control Wheel, this kind of behavior is described as an isolation tactic. Remy had also used male privilege when he ordered Martel to take naps and dictated when she could eat, behaviors reported by Martel's mother.[70] With a previous girlfriend whom he had also physically assaulted, Remy had used coercion and intimidation by threatening to kill her and cutting up her clothes after she told him she was leaving.[71]

When the staff members in Kolb's study defined *empowerment* by saying what it was not (e.g., using intimidation, using coercion and threats, or blaming), they were distinguishing themselves not from other service providers or advocates but from abusers. Engaging in any of these activities was seen as duplicating the dynamics of the abusive relationship, diminishing the client's ability to act on her own. Much of the literature on advocacy for those abused by intimate partners contains similar warnings, focusing especially on the tendency of abusers (as characterized in the Power and Control Wheel) to make "all the big decisions."

It is essential to an empowerment approach, therefore, to provide support and resources while refraining from making decisions for the client. The DVI faculty give a number of reasons for this stance; for example, "co-opting the client's power" does nothing but psychological harm, even if the intentions are good and the client finds the dynamic "familiar and appealing."[72] By "taking away [the client's] ability to think or act independently," which is also a feature of some abusive relationships, an advocate who makes decisions for a client is "further disabling her in her struggle to prevent her abuse."[73] Another reason is that the client herself has more knowledge and control (even if imperfect) of her situation than an advocate ever can.[74] A final reason is that the client is the one who will experience the consequences of any decision. The DVI faculty explain it this way:

The stakes could not be higher—decisions made can literally mean life or death to a woman and/or her loved ones. In this context, the client is the best, and often the only, person to provide the critical information on the danger posed by the batterer, his likely response to a particular course of action, and the implications for her and her children. And, even short of physical violence, the decisions a client makes based on her assessment of her situation will have profound ramifications for her and her family. Every member of her family, including her abusive partner, will feel the impact of her decision—financially, emotionally, and socially. These are not decisions that can be made by an outsider, no matter how well-intentioned.[75]

At the center of this concern is the very real possibility of death: during a single year of the court clinic, two of the program's clients were murdered by their abusers, despite the "very thoughtful decisions" the clients made to keep themselves safe and despite the legal system giving the clients what they asked for.[76] Thus while empowerment is important, so is the client's physical safety.

The twin goals of safety and empowerment create the most difficult challenge for advocates. The challenge usually emerges when a client makes a decision that an advocate thinks will endanger the client's safety. Even in such situations, the DVI faculty argue that the advocate cannot give in to the temptation to tell the client what to do, a temptation that emerges from a desire to be in control as well as an "inappropriate assumption of responsibility."[77] The advocate must instead try to understand the client's choices from *her* point of view. The examples DVI faculty provide are illuminating. Some women, they explain, might endure abuse because they see no way to provide materially for their children if they leave. Others might endure abuse because they have calcu-lated that attempting to leave would mean more extreme violence, perhaps even death. Understanding a client's reasoning, they say, will help advocates understand the constraints informing the clients' decisions.

But these constraints can be underestimated, even by those trained in client empowerment, as sociologists Jennifer L. Dunn and Melissa Powell-Williams found in an interview study of advocates. Dunn and Powell-Williams argue that psychological and individualistic ideologies limit how advocates understand the structural constraints on clients' choices. Remarkably, the advocates they interviewed *never* saw the decision to stay with an abuser as valid.[78] Because of the difficulty in honoring all choices as valid, staff members in Kolb's study engaged in what he calls "steering strategies." These strategies, which subtly influenced clients without appearing directive (either to clients or to themselves), included "planting seeds of doubt" about a client's planned course of action and invoking "the authority of others" to speak in their stead.[79]

When asked whether some of their actions were more directive than empowering, the staff members in Kolb's study would reframe the actions, explaining how they were "ultimately empowering." For example, one advocate, concerned that a client was thinking about returning to an abusive boyfriend, told the client, "I wonder if it is not going to happen again." When Kolb remarked to the advocate that this strategy seemed like steering, the advocate responded "that she thought it was still empowering to encourage a client to reflect or think over her original plans." For Kolb, this reframing was a testament to the centrality of the empowerment philosophy to the staff members' own moral identities as "caring and compassionate peers and allies of victims."[80] This identity stands in stark contrast to cultural representations of the ideal lawyer with which many law students (and lawyers) identify. As Pualani Enos and Lois Kanter explain, their students at the DVI often identified with "directive, hierarchical and individualistic methods of advocacy," despite also "express[ing] an altruistic desire to help battered women."[81]

This description accords with the trope of the heroic lawyer as described in a 1982 study of stereotypes of lawyers held by both lawyers and laypeople. One of three dominant conceptions of lawyers (the other two being trickster and helper), the hero embodies a "highly dramatic role" of a competitor who "takes the initiative in a series of struggles against enemies." Interestingly, laypeople described the heroic lawyer primarily in terms of attitude (what the authors call posture): the hero is "self-confident . . . competitive . . . aggressive . . . and energetic."[82]

Although images of lawyers (in popular culture, at least) now offer a more complex range of typologies than they did in the 1980s,[83] the heroic lawyer remains an important aspirational identity, especially among law students. Several of the students I interviewed for this study embraced at least some of the characteristics of the heroic lawyer before beginning their work with the DVI. Jonathan, for example, spoke of being "someone who is willing to fight for [clients] on their behalf," while Liz wanted to be "a true devil's advocate, really speaking for them as if I were them." Roberto most overtly expressed a desire "to be the hero" and "make the world a perfect place," even though he believed "it's not possible; it's illogical."[84]

For the DVI, one way of disrupting the desire to be a heroic lawyer was to ask students to understand their own subjectivities as emerging from their social and cultural locations. The 2009 manual for court advocates, for example, includes a reprinted article that explains that the values of dominant (white, middle-class, Christian, able-bodied, heterosexual) American culture—including individualism, the belief that success comes through hard work and improvement, and that the nuclear family is the basic unit of society—are not necessarily shared by other cultures. The manual advises "awareness and constant monitoring of . . . one's own values, belief systems and life experience," particularly as these may differ from a client's.[85] Interrogating their own subject positions helped students realize that their viewpoints were partial.

In the manual for advocates, the client is also positioned as a person who is both socially and culturally situated and individually unique. The manual explains, for example, that members of some communities "may feel conflicted about using a racist criminal legal system" and that members of other communities might find divorce or moving to a new community unacceptable.[86] But advocates should not reduce clients to their memberships in these groups or to their experiences of abuse. Instead, advocates need to recognize the client "as a whole person," which means understanding "the abuse in the context of the client's life, rather than defining the client in terms of the abuse."[87]

In the client-empowerment model, seeing the client as a whole person lays the foundation for an attitude of deference. Advocates who imagine clients only in terms of legal categories might more readily assume the position of decision-maker by virtue of their legal expertise. Advocates who recognize that clients, like themselves, have complex lives can more readily see that clients might have goals other than legal ones or that legal resolutions might have burdensome (or dangerous) consequences. They also understand that their clients will be the ones to live with those consequences. For this reason, clients must be the ones to decide which course of action to take. But deferring to clients does not mean that advocates leave them to cope without assistance. Instead, client-empowering advocates provide their own perspectives on the danger posed by an abuser, as well as any possible paths the client might take, so that the client is both better informed and supported.

Like feminist standpoint theorists, the DVI faculty use the metaphor of vision to explain the embodied subjectivity that they hope students will develop: in the client-empowerment model, they write, "the advocate sees the problem through the client's eyes."[88] Students acquired this broader view by learning about domestic violence from those who had experienced it. By listening to many stories, they came to see the uniqueness of each person's circumstances as well as the patterns that highlighted domestic violence as a gendered form of power and control. For students in the hospital program, their first introduction to these stories was at a conference held at the law school, which I discuss in the next chapter.

2

At the Law School | Learning to Recognize the Expertise of Others

In an article about their programs, Domestic Violence Institute (DVI) faculty Pualani Enos and Lois Kanter explain that advocates who see victims of domestic violence as passive and weak may not trust a client's ability to assess her own situation. An advocate with this perception may overestimate her own importance; as they explain, the advocate sees herself as "useful because she has the information, the sophistication, and the power that the client lacks."[1] For this reason, early training was aimed at teaching law students to believe women abused by intimate partners. Without this foundation of belief, would-be advocates might be unable to imagine their potential clients as capable of making their own decisions.

The training discussed in this chapter occurred at an annual one-day conference attended by both students in the hospital program and others interested in advocacy for those abused by intimate partners. As described by Enos and Kanter, the conference "intentionally challenges long-held beliefs and opinions" about domestic violence by "contrasting societal images of abuse with survivors' and advocates' experiences."[2] In 2009, the conference consisted of several workshops and the screening of *Defending Our Lives* (1993), a forty-two-minute documentary film that features testimony from women imprisoned for killing men who had abused them physically, emotionally, and psychologically. The women in the film tell stories of being mistreated not only by their husbands or boyfriends but also by the criminal justice and legal systems. For most of the students in my study, the screening of *Defending Our Lives* and one of the workshops (on helping clients plan for their safety) stood out for their realism and their particularity, or as what one student called "shocking, reality-come-home experiences." This chapter is based on my observations at this conference, which I attended in 2007, 2008, and 2009, as well as interviews conducted with ten students from Boston-area law schools who attended the conference and participated in the hospital program in 2009–2010.[3]

In this chapter, I first describe the problems of perceived character—what rhetoricians call *ethos*—for women abused by intimate partners. I then analyze how *Defending Our Lives* and the safety planning workshop prepared students to believe potential clients by giving students a fuller account of the women's embodied experiences and therefore a window into their situated knowledges. Believing these women meant understanding them as knowing something that only they could know, as being experts in their own lives. *Defending Our Lives* prepared students to believe clients by promoting rhetorical listening as a method of bridging differences in experience and ways of understanding. I then turn to the safety planning workshop, in which participants collaboratively produced descriptions of perpetrator behaviors and their effects, activities that placed the blame for abuse squarely on perpetrators rather than victims.

Through both viewing the film and participating in the workshop, students learned about the embodied experiences of others through activities that often produced visceral reactions in themselves. Students both saw and felt the accumulation of specific (and often gruesome) details that illustrated the difficult conditions under which those in abusive relationships make choices. Together, the film and the workshop helped students understand the complexity of abusive relationships and the very real stakes involved in decisions regarding them. This understanding is crucial to seeing clients as experts in their own lives, a fundamental component of client-empowering advocacy.

The Credibility Problem for Women Abused by Intimate Partners

Feminist rhetoricians have long recognized that *ethos* poses a problem for women speakers. Although *ethos* was theorized by Aristotle as a way of describing how a speaker should create a sense of good character during a speech, he did not account for how preconceptions about speakers might influence their credibility.[4] For women, largely excluded from public speaking for much of history, the first barrier to credibility has been simply being female. As Krista Ratcliffe explains, women's "sex is visibly marked on their bodies" so that merely the "sight of women or the sound of feminists behind the bar or in the pulpit has almost always evoked resistance before they could ever utter a word."[5] Women speaking in public are claiming full personhood in defiance of perceived "defective identities."[6] Character flaws in the defective identities historically ascribed to women include lying and inadequate intellect, both of which construct women as unreliable witnesses to their own or others' experiences. Assumed character flaws are inflected by class and race, with African American women, for example, being seen as even less trustworthy than their white counterparts.[7]

Problems of credibility affect women abused by intimate partners in a number of ways. Many who disclose abuse are not believed by family, friends, clergy, or the police—a fact that abusers can latch on to when exerting control over their victims. Those who do report may produce narratives at odds with traditional notions of truth telling. Women experiencing abuse may not tell their stories at first, hoping that the abuse will end or blaming themselves, and their stories may change as they process their experiences.[8] Organizations that advocate for those abused by intimate partners emphasize that believing someone is one of the most important ways to help. In advice on its website for friends and family, for example, the National Domestic Violence Hotline suggests that what someone in an abusive relationship needs most is "someone who will believe and listen."[9] Another organization, the National Coalition Against Domestic Violence, even suggests that those seeking legal help should ask potential attorneys, "Do you generally believe women who tell you that they have been battered?"[10]

Women who are believed may still be blamed for the violence. They are sometimes seen as responsible for the violence by seeking it out or provoking it. For example, Jared Remy's longtime criminal defense attorney said that Remy and his previous victims of abuse "deserved each other on some level," adding, "They had issues. They pushed buttons. They did things."[11] More frequently, though, women are blamed for staying in the relationship. When women are injured or killed by abusers, the ubiquitous question asked is, "Why didn't she leave?" In 2014, when Baltimore Ravens running back Ray Rice was caught on video assaulting his then fiancée, Janay Palmer, a torrent of media commentators asked this question, prompting the Twitter phenomenon #WhyIStayed.[12] Thousands of people tweeted the reasons they stayed in abusive relationships, a topic that has also been explored by researchers. Many women leave their abusers multiple times.[13] A woman might stay (or return) because she cannot afford to live on her own; because the abuser has threatened her, her children, or her family; because her community or family does not support separation or divorce; or because she loves the abuser and wants to stay in the relationship.[14] Jennifer Martel apparently had been "planning [her] escape" but was staying long enough to "get him help first."[15] In some cases, the woman may feel that she is better off if she stays in the relationship.[16]

The question "Why didn't she leave?" places the blame on the target of abuse rather than the perpetrator, a common feature of discourse about domestic violence. In news reports of violence against women, victims rather than perpetrators are often condemned as deviants who brought the violence on themselves.[17] In legal discourse, women victims are often portrayed as weak, passive, or unsound.[18] In one study, judges considered victims who did not leave their abusers to be intellectually challenged, emotionally flawed, or otherwise responsible for the abuse.[19] Even in briefs and opinions sympathetic to them, women victims are pathologized.[20] To help counteract this tendency in future advocates, law professor Sarah Buel (who speaks in *Defending Our Lives*) urges her students "to refrain from victim-blaming (as in asking 'Why did she stay?') and instead ask, 'Why does a person beat an intimate partner?' and 'Why does the community engage in such high levels of silence, denial and minimization regarding domestic violence?'"[21]

The legal system can be particularly hostile to the claims of women who have killed their abusers, like the women in *Defending Our Lives*. Women who kill husbands (or boyfriends) have historically been treated by the law as categorically different from men who kill their wives.[22] Those who claim self-defense face the challenge of explaining that their force was reasonable, a standard informed by the masculine model of stranger-on-stranger violence. In this model (the prime exemplar being a barroom fight), a person claiming self-defense would need to retreat rather than use force, use force only in proportion to that used by the attacker, and/or use force immediately after an attack rather than delaying. But in situations involving domestic violence, a woman's use of deadly force can't be considered outside of the context of the entire relationship. A woman who kills an abuser is often unable to leave the relationship sooner (i.e., before the only option is deadly force) and has been made to feel powerless and constantly under threat. To equalize the power dynamics, she might use a weapon or rely on surprise by using deadly force when it would seem to others that the abuser posed no immediate threat to her (e.g., when his back was turned or while he was sleeping).[23]

Attorneys for women who kill abusers might not use a self-defense claim because of these difficulties or because the lawyers themselves see the women as irrational.[24] The attorney might advocate that the woman plea insanity instead. Those who do use a self-defense claim sometimes turn to testimony from expert witnesses to help explain the circumstances under which women might kill their abusers. These expert witnesses usually testify about battering or about *battered woman syndrome*, a term coined by psychologist Lenore Walker to explain why women become trapped in violent relationships.[25] While testimony on battered woman syndrome can help achieve an acquittal, it is also problematic. The testimony can pathologize the woman rather than help a judge or jury understand why her behavior could be considered reasonable.[26] Defining the perspectives and behaviors of women in these situations as a "syndrome" implies that their behavior is an abnormal rather than a normal response to ongoing violence, and it faults the victim for developing this response rather than the perpetrator for abusing her. In addition, the syndrome can be used as a fixed set of criteria against which women's behaviors are measured, so that women who behave differently are not seen as having been battered. A woman who fights back, for example, may not appear to be suffering the learned helplessness that is a central part of the syndrome.[27] In addition, because the stereotypes of helplessness and victimization emerge from the experiences and depictions of white women, women of color may not be perceived to exhibit signs of the syndrome. Because African American women are often stereotyped as being angry, for example, judges or juries may be more likely to believe that an African American defendant who killed her abuser acted out of vengeance rather than fear.[28]

Despite its tendency to pathologize victims, battered woman syndrome has been used successfully by defense attorneys, including the counsel of the women whose stories are told in *Defending Our Lives*. These women were members of a support group for female inmates who had killed abusive partners.[29] Although they were not identified as such, five of the women in *Defending Our Lives* were also members of the so-called Framingham Eight, named after the women's prison where they were incarcerated.[30] These women had petitioned the state for early release under new guidelines, enacted in 1991 by newly elected Massachusetts governor William Weld, that allowed battered woman syndrome to be considered by the prison pardons board.[31]

In the next section, I analyze the screening of *Defending Our Lives* for students in the DVI programs. When introducing the film to students, then director Lois Kanter said it was "the best introduction to domestic violence" that she knew of because it illustrated the circumstances constraining victims' choices. For those unfamiliar with domestic violence, these choices could seem counterintuitive. As I explain next, the film bolstered the credibility of those abused by intimate partners by encouraging students to listen rhetorically to their stories.

Rhetorical Listening in *Defending Our Lives*

In *Defending Our Lives*, four women give detailed accounts of being abused by boyfriends or husbands before eventually killing them. The forty-two-minute documentary has particular resonance for advocates in Massachusetts, as it features women from the commonwealth and was produced and directed by local filmmakers. The film won several awards, including an Academy Award (1994) for best short documentary, and has been shown in the United Nations, the US Senate and House, state legislatures, museums, police academies, and other venues.[32] It is widely shown in university courses on domestic violence, sociology, and women's studies. At the time the film was made, one of the original Framingham Eight had been released; by the time of its Oscar, five more were awaiting release or had been released, and another was released a few months later. After the women's release, some spoke regularly at screenings of the film and at forums on domestic abuse and violence against women, including one who traveled to Denmark to speak at a United Nations conference on social issues.[33] Their stories were also the subject of an hour-long report in 1998 on the ABC News program *Turning Point*.[34]

The women tell their stories from inside prison cells, recounting their mistreatment not just by male partners but also by the criminal justice system. All were all given long initial sentences, their convictions based on male-centered notions of reasonable behavior and self-defense. Shannon Booker, whose boyfriend had beaten her with a billy club and thrown her down stairs, shot him during a fight. Lisa Grimshaw, who endured years of sexual assault and physical terror by her husband, waited nearby while two of her coworkers beat him with baseball bats. Although Patricia Hennessy had left her husband after he tried to run down her and their son with his van, he continued to harass and threaten her; she shot him when he came to pick up their son for a visitation. Eugenia Moore's ex-boyfriend stalked her and threatened repeatedly to kill her; she stabbed him after he attacked her in her car.

Law students viewed *Defending Our Lives* at the beginning of a day-long conference designed to introduce them to domestic violence before they began their work in the hospital program. Before the conference, most of the students knew little about domestic violence and few had heard first-person testimonies of the sort presented in the film. The film thus played an important role in shaping how they would approach the hospital program. Most significantly, the film encouraged rhetorical listening, the foundation for client empowerment that they would employ in their roles as interviewers at the hospital. By listening rhetorically to the film, students came to understand domestic violence as a complex social problem rather than an idiosyncratic feature of some interpersonal relationships.

Seeing domestic violence as a complex social problem helped bolster the credibility of the women in the film. Importantly, all ten students I interviewed praised the character of the women profiled. Although the women were in prison for killing their abusers, the film does not focus narrowly on this single act. Instead, it shows the broader context within which they acted, establishing each woman's *ethos* as a *location* rather than as an expression of individual character. As rhetorician Nedra Reynolds explains, rhetors "construct and establish *ethos* when they say explicitly 'where they are coming from.'"[35] Liz, a student who had been in a controlling relationship herself, located the women's *ethos* within a patriarchal culture, saying, "I was so impressed with their character. . . . The stereotype of abused women is someone who is meek and fearful, and these women obviously were scared, but . . . you could feel like they're real people, like this could happen to women anywhere."

Defending Our Lives focuses on the broad context of domestic violence by promoting two related "moves" that Ratcliffe has associated with rhetorical listening. The first is the creation of identifications across not only commonalities but also differences, allowing for communication across cultural divides. Such identifications are crucial when advocating for those on the margins of powerful institutions. The second move is the analysis of not only claims (what a person says) but also cultural logics (the epistemological frameworks within which claims are made).[36] In the film, this move is accomplished by placing each woman's experience into a social and cultural context rather than a narrowly legal one. By expanding the scene of intimate abuse, the film helped students understand the actions of the abused women, even if they could not imagine taking those same actions themselves, thus redefining what counts as reasonable behavior. These redefinitions are possible because the film values the women's embodied knowledge as much as the expertise held by professionals in the legal and criminal justice systems. A woman in an abusive relationship knows truths about her situation that outsiders do not necessarily see, such as how likely her abuser is to do her serious harm.

As a documentary, *Defending Our Lives* is a particularly effective pedagogical tool in this context. Documentary film is what film theorist Bill Nichols calls a "discourse of sobriety"—that is, a discourse whose credibility relies on the perception of its "relation to the real as direct, immediate, transparent."[37] A number of the law students commented on the power of this immediacy. For Gretchen, the film made it feel "like they were in the room with us, like having someone say, 'This happened to me.'" Both Gretchen and Kelly thought the film "put a face on" a problem that they understood abstractly. As Kelly explained, "It's not a snapshot, soundbite. It's an actual person's story." The details of these stories are what stood out for Liz: "I don't think you hear about that . . . some of the abuse, how extreme it was. You just don't hear about that or you don't think about it. Even now, I don't feel like you see that in the news often." Hearing not just about the abuse but about their "regular lives, what they were doing," helped Liz feel "connected with them . . . on a very human level."

The law students identified with the women in *Defending Our Lives* in two ways. In some cases, the students sensed having something in common with the women, what rhetorician Kenneth Burke calls consubstantiality.[38] But more often, the students identified across differences while coming to understand the cultural logics underpinning the women's claims. As Ratcliffe explains, this kind of identification is based on discourse (i.e., cultural logics) rather than substance (i.e., common ground).[39] *Defending Our Lives* promotes this kind of understanding through the women's narratives, which paint a picture of the dynamics of domestic violence. Focusing on the broad contexts within which these women acted, rather than the immediate circumstances of the abusers' deaths, allowed the students to see the women's ultimate actions as something reasonable. As Jonathan explained, "I understood why they felt that they had to do what they did, and in that way, it showed that women who are abused and kill their abusers—it is not an isolated thing, and it happens for a reason."

For the law students, rhetorical listening was encouraged in the film by what Burke calls the scene-act ratio: the *scene* of domestic violence controlled how the students interpreted the *act* of killing an abuser. Ratios, for Burke, are a way of understanding how a given discourse frames (and therefore constructs) a particular reality. Ratios consist of two elements from what Burke called the pentad (scene, act, agent, agency, and purpose), a set of terms used to describe statements about human motivation.[40] The scene-act ratio can be especially powerful; changing the scope (or "circumference") of the scene within which an act is viewed affects how one views the act itself.[41] In *Defending Our Lives*, the act of killing an abuser is situated not just within a physical space (such as a bedroom) or a personal one (such as a marriage) but in relation to social and cultural institutions such as extended families, workplaces, and the criminal justice system.

Defending Our Lives portrays the actions in these settings as so brutal that the students were not surprised when the abusers were killed, an effect achieved because an act's quality can be inferred from the quality of the scene.[42] Although the violence suffered by women at the hands of their abusers signals serious consequences, the film does not portray the abusers as deserving death, and it does not portray each woman as vigilante—as judge, jury, and executioner. Instead, after the women have exhausted other means of keeping themselves safe, the abusers' deaths appear inevitable. While the women do carry out the final act of killing their abusers, students saw them as substitutes for other agents of justice. As Kathy explained, "It didn't feel like, at the point that it got to, that they had a choice other than what they did." She believed that earlier interventions could have prevented the men's deaths, as did Jessica, who thought the film illustrated how changing the system could help women "get out of the situation before it reached that point."

This sense of inevitability is a feature of the scene-act ratio, which makes choices seem reduced by circumstances.[43] For the women in *Defending Our Lives*, their choices are eliminated generally by the failure of society to condemn domestic violence and specifically by the failure of the police to protect them, even as they tried to protect themselves. As Liz said, "I think a lot of these women tried to call the police, use the courts. Maybe that's why I felt proud of them by the end because . . . what else do you do?" The irony, of course, is that the women end up imprisoned by the state instead of their abusers. This irony, as well as the inevitability of the women's actions, is emphasized by the interview settings: all four are filmed within prison, with window bars and locked doors clearly visible. In the end, students were left contemplating not the justice of killing an abuser but the injustice of the system's failure to help women protect themselves from abuse.

Significantly, the scene of domestic violence in *Defending Our Lives* is both a collective and an individualized experience, epitomized by the role of Meekah Scott. Scott is introduced early on as a community educator; toward the end, students learn that she was out on appeal after being sentenced to eight to twelve years for killing her abuser. Scott does not tell her own story but recites the names, ages, and means of death of twenty Massachusetts women killed by their abusers within an eleven-month period. This recitation occurs at regular intervals throughout the film and is accompanied by images of body bags and funeral caskets.

During this part of the film, Kathy remembered thinking, "How prevalent is this? Why aren't more people outraged?" For this student, who had no prior first- or secondhand experience with intimate abuse, Scott's recitation brought to light the enormity of the problem. While the names that Scott recites memorialize the individual women, the sparse details and similarities of their experiences and the accompanying visual images create a collective drumbeat. Her recitation affected other students deeply as well. As Kim recalled, "She only did about a year's worth . . . not even a year's worth. I wanted her to just keep going because I wanted to hear . . . if that was one year. I wanted to hear more. All of these people in all of these communities and all these places." Liz felt especially affected because the towns were local, saying, "I grew up in Massachusetts, and hearing the names of the towns . . . and . . . where they lived and what their names were [was] . . . very jarring."

The scene of domestic violence as both collective and individualized extends to the stories of Shannon Booker, Lisa Grimshaw, Patricia Hennessy, and Eugenia Moore. Each woman, still in prison, tells her story in detail so that the students come to understand her actions, yet the stories are intertwined so that their commonalities are emphasized. In the first part, all four women share how their relationships began and how the abuse began. They then describe the escalation of the abuse and their efforts to stay safe. Finally, the women describe killing their abusers and then explain their trials and imprisonment. Jonathan, who trained and worked as a journalist before going to law school, said that he paid particular attention to this narrative sequencing, admiring how the film "bounced back and forth from one woman to the next to the next to the next, and it slowly built each woman's story and involved you in their story, and it progressively did that for each woman, so that by the time you got to the end, you really understood . . . why they felt that they had to do what they did."

This narrative sequencing mirrors the tension in advocacy for women abused by intimate partners, and feminist theory more generally, between the particular and the general. The telling of individual women's stories was central to feminist consciousness raising of the late 1960s and early 1970s, which gave rise to the domestic violence movement.[44] This practice is now seen by postmodern feminists as a way to avoid essentialism because it highlights women's differences as rooted in the particularities of their everyday lives. Yet it was through consciousness raising that women first gleaned that their experiences were not particular to them; they began to realize that other women were being abused and that domestic violence was linked to patriarchal social and cultural institutions.[45] Generalizing from women's individual experiences was important for collective action. Highlighting both particularities and generalities is also essential for feminist legal advocacy. Generalizing allows for the creation of categories that are both theoretically insightful and strategically useful.[46] The concept of the "battered woman," for example, has helped attorneys identify the experience as a common one with pervasive features. Yet because the term also reduces women in this situation to that experience alone and is accompanied by negative stereo-types about helplessness and victimization, relying on it (or related terms, such as *battered woman syndrome*) can signify to legal decision-makers (e.g., judges and juries) that women in this situation are all the same.[47]

In some ways, the film works against this homogenization by encouraging students to listen metonymically, a mode of rhetorical listening that draws on the rhetorical figure of metonymy, which describes something by naming something closely associated with it.[48] As an example of metonymy, "Madison Avenue" is often used to refer to the advertising industry as a whole because many advertising agencies are located on that street in New York. Madison Avenue and the advertising industry are associated with one another but not identical. As a figure that emphasizes association rather than common substance, meton-ymy can help avoid the kind of stereotyping implied by the "battered woman" label. The narrative structure of the film emphasizes how the women are associ-ated because of the common experience of abuse, but the details of the indi-vidual stories work against homogenization. In other ways, however, the film contributes to the stereotype that domestic violence is a problem only in hetero-sexual relationships. Although one of the Framingham Eight had killed her female partner, her story is not told. The film also does not address the experi-ences of other women in same-sex relationships or of male victims.[49]

The topos of sameness/difference that operates among the women in the film also operates between the women and students as they viewed the film. Especially in the beginning, the women in *Defending Our Lives* are depicted as quite ordinary and engaging in relationships that appear normal, encouraging students to identify with the women based on shared cultural expectations about relationships. The students heard the women's stories about the begin-nings of their relationships and the beginnings of abuse. Each woman describes the start of her relationship as ordinary and the man as normal, even attentive and generous. Any student who had not been in a controlling or violent relationship could imagine herself or himself in a similar situation because the relationships don't show the warning signs of domestic violence. Hannah, who had no prior experience with intimate abuse, noted that each future abuser in the film "starts off as any boyfriend" and that the relationship is "healthy and normal at the beginning." Liz elaborated,

> I can identify with them because to me, they seemed like regular women, all of them. I mean, obviously [they all had] different backgrounds and class and stuff like that, but to me, especially the part where they talk about getting into the relationship....I think maybe my perception is you can identify a batterer right away. Or there's like warning signs you should be able to see. For a lot of these women, they were like, "Oh, it was my high school guy I dated or I knew since I was ten and we got married and it was fine." That may be where I identified with them....You think you know somebody and then suddenly you're just stuck. So I think that can happen to anybody....These are real people. They're not just women you hear about in the newspaper....The woman who was a bus driver—she had kids, she had this career, she was very proud of it, and I want to have kids. I want to have a career. All these things—and look at this man who can just totally turn her life upside down. So for me it was like, well, that could be me. It could be my friends. It could be anybody.

This kind of identification is based on commonality. The collective depiction of the relationships' beginnings—one told right after the other—highlights the commonalities in the stories and their proximity to ordinary relationships.

As it progresses, the film promotes identification based not on commonality but on difference. While some of the law students may have identified with individual women in the film at some level, none of them had experienced what the stories narrate: killing an abuser. The film encouraged students to attend not only to what a person says (or does)—that is, the person's claims—but to the cultural logics that underpin those claims. As Ratcliffe explains, listening only to the claims makes it too easy to dismiss the ones that differ from one's own beliefs. However, paying attention to the cultural logics underlying those claims means trying to recognize the world views within which a person operates. Understanding cultural logics means that the listener can comprehend how a person comes to make certain claims or take particular actions. *Defending Our*

Lives encouraged students to pay attention to these cultural logics by focusing on the scene of domestic violence, or the larger context that informs the women's acts of killing their abusers.

At first, students encountered a relatively narrow scene for domestic violence—namely, the relationship between the woman and her abuser. The escalation and severity of the violence is shocking. Lisa Grimshaw's husband raped her with objects, sodomized her, tied her up, knocked out her teeth, and threatened to cut her baby from her abdomen. Eugenia Moore's boyfriend stalked her, attacked her during her route as a bus driver, and told her repeatedly that he would kill her. Shannon Booker's boyfriend beat her, threw her down stairs, and played Russian roulette by putting a gun into her mouth and pulling the trigger. Patricia Hennessy's husband hit her in the abdomen when she was pregnant. These descriptions are placed alongside photographs of the same women with scars and bruises and photographs of other women with horrific injuries such as stab wounds and swollen, bloodied faces, as well as a litany of abuses with which narrator Sarah Buel begins the film:

> They are punched, kicked. They're beaten while trying to hold onto their babies. They are strangled, choked, burned with cigarettes, doused with kerosene and lighter fluid and set on fire. They are run over by cars and trucks. They have their teeth knocked out with hammers. They are stabbed with everything from knives to ice picks to screwdrivers—anything that penetrates. Their children are forced to watch their assaults and torture, and they are often tied up and forced to watch the torture and molestation of their own children.

The photographs, along with Buel's summary, serve as independent corroboration of the women's testimony.

Many of the law students had visceral responses to these depictions. Kathy reported crying. Kim, whose mother had been brutally beaten by her father and who had worked as a victim witness advocate in a local district attorney's office, had to fight crying. Kelly, who had no prior experience with domestic violence, compared the effect to being hit by a train. Gretchen, who likewise had no first- or secondhand knowledge of abuse, admitted to feeling "almost nauseated by the injuries," saying, "Some of the things they did, there's a physiological response. ...I think it's natural for some of that to seep in and have a physiological response of nausea. It's just so wrong; it's so much pain." She was relieved to be given a few minutes to debrief with someone else immediately after the screening because "it was definitely the kind of thing where you find yourself holding your breath, kind of in shock."

Students then saw an expansion of the scene of domestic violence, as the middle of each woman's story narrates the failure of the police to protect her, showing that the women are victimized not only by their abusers but also by the system. For Lisa Grimshaw, who had multiple restraining orders against her abuser, the police stopped coming when she called, and the criminal charges brought against him when they did come (attempted murder, assault and bat- tery with a dangerous weapon) never resulted in a conviction. For Patricia Hennessy, the police arrived after her husband had broken her nose and would not arrest him because they had not witnessed the violence. The police's inaction emboldened her abuser, who gave her a worse beating after they left.

Students saw a broadened scene of domestic violence that included the criminal justice and legal systems as well as the intimate relationship. This wider scope helped create a moral order that placed the abused women on one side and their abusers, the police, and the legal system on the other. It also helped dispel the stereotype of women as passively accepting abuse or as incapable of helping themselves. The problem is not that the women lack strategies for survival but that the institutions that are supposed to help do not. Each woman in the film attempts to leave her abuser; each tries to enlist the help of institutions such as the police. Yet the police treat the violence against them differently than violence between strangers. Eugenia Moore explains the reaction of the police when her ex-boyfriend attacked her on the city bus she was driving:

> When the police came, I said, "Arrest him, arrest him, he just attacked me!" I was in hysterics. The guy said, "Wait a minute, wait a minute, he says he's your boyfriend." I said, "My boyfriend? What's that got to do with it? The man just attacked me.". . . "Well, we didn't see anything." They didn't see anything—they're the police. . . . In the meantime, Alfred's standing back there, joking around, laughing. It was all a big joke to him. I couldn't believe what was happening. I was embarrassed, I was so ashamed—this was on the job. It had been on the streets before, people had intervened, but this was on the job. I didn't know if I was going to get fired or what.

Students who were unaware of how domestic violence is treated socially, culturally, and institutionally might not have known of the difficulties—material as well as psychological—of keeping oneself safe or that leaving an abuser doesn't always stop the abuse.[50] Before watching the film, many of the law students had a neutral or positive view of how police handled domestic violence. While several doubted that police departments prioritized domestic violence, several others believed the opposite—that is, that police officers were particularly sympathetic to victims, especially women victims. Only Kim, who had extensive personal and professional experience with intimate abuse, saw police as mostly unsympathetic and even hostile to victims. After watching the film, most of the students felt shocked by the behaviors of the police, with many wondering whether responses had improved in the years since the film was made. (Though not recounted in *Defending Our Lives*, Sarah Buel observed firsthand how the parole officers for Grimshaw and Booker repeatedly abused and humiliated them, called them liars, and threatened to recommend that they be returned to prison.[51])

Aligning the police with the abusers prompted in students not only identification with these women but also division from the criminal justice system. The final part of the women's stories links the criminal justice system to the judicial process, with which many law students identified, by illustrating how the women were mistreated by the courts. After shooting her boyfriend with his gun during a fight, Booker was charged with first-degree murder. At the police station, she says, no one seemed concerned for her well-being, despite the fact that she was bleeding and badly bruised. She was sentenced to eight to fifteen years. Moore was convicted of second-degree murder and sentenced to life in prison after the judge refused to hear evidence about battered woman syndrome.

Students understood that the harms suffered by both Grimshaw and Hennessy were magnifications of the harms inflicted by their abusers. While Grimshaw's husband left her tied to a bed for hours, the criminal justice system kept her in a small cell for years; while Hennessy's husband had threatened to take her son away, the court did so after she was sentenced to prison for manslaughter.[52] These accounts are bolstered by Sarah Buel, reporting in the film that women who kill abusers "have higher initial bails set . . . are detained longer, and ultimately have longer sentences than any other type of defendant, including serial rapists and murderers." Law student Liz took the failure of the system personally, saying, "I take a lot of pride in our legal system because this is what I want to do, and to think that it is doing such a disservice to women is upsetting. It's really shameful. It's embarrassing. If you're an attorney, you're like, 'Yeah, this is what we do. We throw women in jail who were beaten for fifteen years for finally acting in self-defense.' Which is exactly what they did."

In killing their abusers, the women were seen by students not only as abandoned (or worse) by the system but as assuming its role of protector. In this way, the women were placed on a higher moral plane than both the abusers and the criminal justice system. The women not only endured unspeakable horrors; they also became agents of justice as the result of an epic battle that only one person could survive. Both Hennessy and Booker say that "it was me or him," and Moore notes of her ex-boyfriend that "he came to murder me. It just so happened that I put the final blow to him instead of him putting the final blow to me." All the students said they understood why the women felt they had to kill their abusers, with half of the students explicitly saying that the women were justified. Kathy, who had no prior experience with domestic violence, remarked, "It didn't feel like . . . [the women] had a choice other than what they did. It did feel like, if you could have intervened sooner, there might have been a different outcome." Roberto, whose mother had been abused by his father, had a similar reaction, saying, "They did what they had to do, so good for them. But I wish they didn't have to go to jail for it." The women did not willingly take on this ultimate defense of their lives; instead, it was thrust upon them by the system's failure, as Hennessy explains: "The police should have protected me, the courts should have protected me, and they didn't, and here I sit." For Grimshaw too "there didn't have to be a death, and it didn't have to be me in prison. . . . It didn't have to be this way."

Yet these epic battles do not fit the model of stranger-on-stranger violence that informs traditional legal definitions of self-defense. The deaths of Moore's and Booker's abusers adhere most closely to the model: both involved a physical struggle in which harm seemed imminent. Moore's ex-boyfriend stalked her, attacking her in her car. Although Shannon Booker killed her abuser in their home, his death also occurred during a struggle. After a fight, Booker hid her boyfriend's gun under their bed to keep it away from him; soon afterward, in another fight, she pulled the gun out and shot him. In contrast, the deaths of Grimshaw's and Hennessy's abusers occurred when the threat of violence did not seem imminent. Lisa Grimshaw lured her husband to the woods, where two coworkers beat him to death with baseball bats, and Patricia Hennessy shot her ex-husband when he came to pick up their son for a visitation. Their deaths challenge commonly accepted notions of reasonable behavior.

Given these immediate circumstances, it is not surprising that Moore (whose act most closely fits the traditional model of self-defense) was the first to be released early and that Hennessy (whose act least resembles it) never was. (Significantly, in Lisa Grimshaw's case, the pardons board was split along gender lines, with its three men voting against early release and its three women voting in favor. Then governor William Weld did not rule on the question of a pardon, instead advising Grimshaw to apply for early parole, which she received.[53]) Moore, in fact, was the first to test the new prison pardons board guidelines. According to her attorney Susan Howards, "If Eugenia didn't make it, none of the women would have made it."[54] Law student Kathy remarked, "I just couldn't believe she was in jail. It wasn't like he was lying there and she walked in and shot him. It happened in the midst of an altercation where he was trying to kill her."

Defending Our Lives deemphasizes the differences in the abusers' deaths by downplaying agency, or how the women carried out the killings. In this way, the film helped students identify with the women as a group, despite the fact that the deaths of two of the men did not fit the standard model of self-defense. The stories of the abusers' deaths also highlight the immediate context rather than the women's roles. Grimshaw's story, for example, emphasizes the role of her two coworkers. They asked her if she wanted them to "take care of this for [her]," they suggested beating him up, and when the beating began, she ran away. Killing him does not seem to be her intent; of the plan to beat up her husband, she says, "I don't know what I was thinking." And killing him does not seem to be her coworkers' intent: when they returned to the car after the attack, one asked the other, "Why did you keep hitting him?" Law student Alexandra, whose family had sheltered a friend trying to leave her violent husband, explicitly compared Grimshaw's case to Moore's:

> Obviously [these women killed in] self-defense, right? . . . One of [the cases] was clear. The guy came up behind her, and she came up and stabbed him. I can't believe that it wouldn't be self-defense. I haven't taken criminal law yet but . . . the one about the guy in the woods, her story was so much more graphic about all the things he did to her over the years. . . . I don't believe in the death penalty, and you can't kill people to solve your problems, but I totally believe if someone's hurting you, then you have the right to defend yourself. I sympathize with these women, and I don't think they should be spending their lives in prison.

Note how Alexandra did not compare the immediate circumstances of each abuser's death. Instead, she compared the immediate circumstances of the death of Moore's boyfriend ("the guy came up behind her") to the broader context of Grimshaw's life with her husband ("all the things he did to her over the years"). Alexandra saw both as justifiable self-defense because of the hurt inflicted by the abusers, regardless of when it occurred temporally in relation to their deaths.

Emphasizing the scene of domestic violence influenced how the law students identified with the women in the film. Some law students tried to imagine how they would *act* in similar circumstances: Liz, who had been in a controlling relationship herself, wondered, "What would I do if that was my son? If it was some man who's been hitting me for the last ten years?" Roberto, whose father had abused his mother, was more certain: "If I felt that my kid was in danger, I would probably react the same way. You have to protect what's important to you." Others imagined how they might *feel*. Kelly, who had no first- or second-hand experience with intimate abuse, said, "It's incredibly hard to imagine yourself in that situation. . . .So while not putting yourself in their shoes, you can understand how it feels to feel that way." In each of these cases, the student identified with the women in the film because their actions made sense given their cultural logics. The students examined not just the women's actions but the material conditions and belief systems within which these actions were situated.

The Rhetoric of Blame in Lethality Assessment

A workshop following the screening of *Defending Our Lives* aimed at teaching what the conference program called "the most critical aspect of advocacy for victims: the safety of victims and their children." For the DVI, the victim's safety is one of the primary reasons for a client-empowerment approach to advocacy. Because the client knows the abuser best and will feel the impact of any decisions, she must make decisions herself.[55] When adopting a client-empowerment approach, the advocate provides information and additional perspectives to help the client make these decisions. In domestic violence, much of that information is demographic: an advocate would know about patterns of abuse and risk across situations and populations that an individual victim of domestic violence might not know. Sharing that information with clients can help them understand their situations in a broader framework.

The safety workshop at the conference was held in a law school classroom with about thirty participants. It focused on three topics: the actions of abusers, the effects of these actions on their targets of abuse, and factors that increased the risk of death at the hands of an abuser (called lethality assessment). Like the film, the workshop painted a picture of the complex, embodied reality of abuse and its consequences. Law student Gretchen said that the workshop was "really hard, especially on the heels of seeing the movie, having the faces of the women suffering through these things fresh in your mind." For Gretchen, the details of abuse in the workshop were "not some grand, abstract idea" but instead descriptions of what "women right now" were currently going through.

The primary pedagogical tools were three tables drawn by the workshop's facilitators on whiteboards at the front of the classroom. The information in the tables—one on the actions of abusers (table 1), one on the effects on their targets of abuse (table 2), and one on lethality assessment (table 3)—was produced collaboratively through discussion between the facilitators and the workshop participants. Participants consisted of both novices regarding the problem of domestic violence (such as the students beginning the hospital program) and experts from the community. Those with no prior experience with domestic violence could contribute by virtue of having just watched *Defending Our Lives*, while those with some knowledge could contribute without necessarily disclosing the source of their knowledge. Kelly appreciated this mix of people, as she felt she was learning from people who really understood how domestic violence "plays out in day-to-day life."

All three of the tables produced in the workshop were examples of what the Greeks called *ekphrasis*, or "descriptive language, bringing what is portrayed clearly before the sight."[56] In the ancient sophistic pedagogical tradition, *ekphrasis* was one of a series of exercises (*progymnasmata*) designed to prepare students to compose speeches.[57] Students in this tradition generally went through the exercises sequentially, reaching *ekphrasis* toward the end. Its placement near exercises such as encomium (a composition praising the virtues of a person or thing) and vituperation (a composition attacking the vices of a person or thing) suggests that *ekphrasis* was particularly useful for rhetorics of praise and blame, called epideictic rhetoric.[58] The description at the core of this workshop served a similar purpose. By focusing squarely on the actions of abusers, the workshop functioned epideictically to blame *them* rather than their victims.

In Aristotle's taxonomy, epideictic rhetoric is one of three rhetorical genres, exemplified by the funeral oration, although the techniques of praise or blame can be used in other types of speeches. Its social function, as explained by rhetorical theorists Chaim Perelman and Lucie Olbrechts-Tyteca, is to "increase the intensity of adherence to certain values."[59] By amplifying shared values, epideictic rhetoric can help unite a community. Education itself can be seen as epideictic, as it uses praise and blame to teach reasoning and emotions that are "appropriate within the orthodoxy which the teacher represents."[60]

Embodied participation in pedagogical practices can inculcate in students values particular to a profession, as T. Kenny Fountain demonstrates in his study of gross anatomy classes. Through interaction with multimodal objects and displays in these labs, students in Fountain's study acquired a sensitivity to "the simultaneous biological value and humanity of the body."[61] Similarly, the tables produced in the lethality assessment workshop inculcated law students into shared values about responsibility: the perpetrator is the one responsible for the abuse.

Table 1 focused most squarely on the abuser's actions. It started, in the leftmost column, with physical attacks, the most obvious of abusive actions. The first items to be added to that list were also the most obvious and perhaps the most common (punching, hitting, slapping, etc.), with more violent and extreme acts added later (drowning, suffocating, injecting). Many of the acts depicted in the other columns may have been surprising for those unfamiliar with domestic violence. Although the table was intended to illustrate the range of acts that a number of abusers could commit, for Gretchen, the visual effect created a "Frankenstein['s] monster of a man who is abusing pets and controlling money and jealous and [abusing children] . . . and whatever else." Gretchen knew that "very few people are all of [those] things," but "seeing it all up on the board, in one place and painting a picture," compelled her to see a composite. The composite functioned as an epitome, amplifying the emotional impact.

Gretchen had a physiological reaction to this activity, saying, "[It] made me sick to my stomach." Like other student participants, the thought of pet abuse hit her especially hard. Alexandra explained why: "To kill a pet is just so incredibly evil. . . . Of course, I value an animal's life, [but] not as much as a person's life. It's more like the idea behind it is, 'You're next.' That's pretty serious. It's way more serious than breaking a plate." Including the killing of pets in this table of abusive actions is one way that this activity broadened the definition of abuse well beyond the legal definition in most states. Massachusetts law, for example, recognizes only physical harm (as well as threatening or attempting it) or forced sexual activity as legal grounds for obtaining abuse prevention orders. This

Table 1   Abusive Actions

Physical	Psychological/ Emotional	Economic	Sexual	Using Children
Punching, hitting, slapping, throwing, pushing, cutting, stabbing, strangling, hitting with a car, biting, kicking, shooting, restraining, burning (with cigarettes, chemicals, irons), pinching, scratching, drowning, suffocating, injecting, forcing to eat, avoiding leaving marks that will be seen by others.	Depriving of sleep, calling names, isolating, becoming jealous, teasing, humiliating in public, threatening, attacking self-esteem, controlling, putting down family and friends, forcing to quit school or work, depriving of social interaction, preventing from driving, taking away phone, monitoring, stalking, constant texting/emailing, destroying property, hurting or killing pets, smothering with attention, threatening suicide, interfering with social relationships, lying, invalidating feelings, making constant demands.	Preventing from working or going to school, jeopardizing job by making her late or miss work, calling employer, refusing to support financially, giving an allowance/ doling out money, preventing access to information about finances, ruining credit, not paying rent, gambling, spending money on drugs, spending her paycheck. If she is an immigrant, threatening to report to immigration, preventing from learning English, or misrepresenting opportunities for work or school.	Breast or genital mutilation, raping with objects, forced oral sex, forced intercourse, forced anal sex, sex with others, erotic asphyxiation, sex in front of others, withholding sex, bringing home STDs, taking videos or photographs of sex acts.	Threatening to take them away, telling her that no one will think she's a good mother, turning children against her, hurting children, threatening to kill children, kidnapping, threatening to call child protective services. Plus physical, emotional, economic, and sexual abuse against children.

expanded definition of abuse could help would-be advocates see the value and limitations of legal remedies. It could also help them see abuse in the "power and control" framework described in chapter 1.

Table 2 had two main rhetorical functions. First, it implicitly linked the abusive actions from table 1 to impacts on victims in a cause-effect relationship. A victim of abuse doesn't simply acquire broken bones or loss of hearing; those physical impacts are a direct result of the abusive actions of the perpetrator.

Table 2   Impacts on Victims of Abuse

Physical	Psychological/Emotional	Social/Economic
Death, broken bones, chronic pain, incapacity/disability, disfigurement, scarring, loss of teeth, bruises, mental impairment, loss of brain function, loss of balance, loss of hearing, loss of eyesight, incontinence, sleeplessness, miscarriage, panic attacks.	Anxiety, eating problems, attention deficit disorder, post-traumatic stress disorder, withdrawal, nightmares, paranoia, isolation, addiction, depression, dissociative behavior, intrusive thoughts, memory impairment, suicidal thoughts, homicidal thoughts, manipulation, anger, distrustfulness, bitterness, fear, vengefulness, hysteria, inappropriate affect, self-blame, self-denial, self-mutilation, risky behavior.	Behavior that is annoying, needy, self-centered, defiant, uncooperative, self-destructive, oppositional, hypersensitive, passive. Poverty, dependence, loss of children, loss of support structures.

Second, it provided explicit context for any behaviors that might impair the credibility of victims. As the workshop leaders explained, knowing that a perpetrator's actions can lead a victim to addiction or an uncooperative attitude, for example, could help would-be advocates avoid blaming clients and suggest appropriate support. Descriptions of victims as "annoying" or "hypersensitive," while perhaps unsettling, serve an important pedagogical function. As the student manual explains, many who work with victims "have come to view angry and demanding victims as aggressors in partner conflicts, unwilling to cooperate with efforts to protect them, or otherwise undeserving of assistance from the social welfare or legal systems."[62] Describing unattractive behaviors is the first step toward understanding them as possible effects of abuse rather than causes.

Table 3 amplified the most important value of this community of advocates: the victim's safety. Several of the law students had vivid memories of the facilitator emphasizing which of the "batterer-generated risks" (e.g., pet abuse, sadistic sexual abuse, and threats of suicide or homicide) were the biggest predictors that the victim would die at the hands of the abuser. As Hannah recalled, the facilitator "circled [pet abuse] like five times and said, 'This right here, this is a big sign.'" Although Hannah said that she would not have immediately thought of pet abuse as an indicator of lethality, she stated, "Once it was put on the board, I'm like, okay, that makes sense." Liz and Jonathan were similarly surprised to see pet abuse as an indicator of lethality. Liz hadn't even imagined people capable of threatening, kicking, or killing pets. Both of them saw this

Table 3   Lethality Assessment

Life-Generated Risks	Batterer-Generated Risks
Poverty: lack of stable housing, lack of stable income, lack of financial independence or cash on hand, low education or job skills, low employment or underemployment	Mental illness of abuser: unpredictable behavior, self-medication through substance abuse, stopping prescribed medications, suicidal threats, homicidal threats
Immigrant status: lack of green card, inability to speak English, hesitancy to speak to authorities, no trust in police	History of violence: pet abuse, prior restraining orders, willingness to engage in violent behavior
	Access to guns
Culture: high tolerance for violence against women, lack of tolerance for divorce, insularity	Threats: specific vs. general, frequency, client's assessment, whether accompanied by beatings or displays of violence, whether he talks about what he's done to others
Disability/age: dangerous level of dependency, immobility, access to health care only through abuser	
	Reputation for violence
Mental illness: lack of credibility, lack of access to health care	Relationship behaviors: jealousy, obsessiveness, financial control, stalking, isolation/imprisonment, taking away phone, paranoia/accusations
Substance abuse	
History of abuse	Property damage: photographs, items with sentimental value
Presence of children: custody issues, potential for kidnapping, financial support, difficulty in moving	Severity of beatings, whether woman is pregnant
Employment/schooling: abuser knows location of workplace or school	Enlisting help of others in abuse
	Child abuse/molestation
	Sexual violence/degradation

new knowledge as useful when working with future clients to help them assess their risk.

Table 3 also explicitly avoided blaming the victim, as the first column is titled "Life-Generated Risks" rather than "Victim-Generated Risks." The information in this column situated those abused by intimate partners within a complex web of cultural and social institutions, effectively demonstrating constraints on their agency. Those who lack stable housing or income are at more risk for being killed by a partner, as are those in cultures with a high tolerance for violence against women. Through this table, especially in combination with the others, would-be advocates could clearly imagine many answers to the question, "Why didn't she just leave?"

These activities, along with the viewing of *Defending Our Lives*, inculcated students into a central value of client-empowering advocacy—believing the victim—by introducing them to the world views of those whose voices are often ignored, discounted, or misunderstood by legal actors. These activities made these realities accessible by encouraging attentiveness not just to the discrete acts usually of concern to the law but also to the broader contexts within which these acts are situated.

But watching the film and participating in the workshop didn't necessarily teach students another central value of client-empowering advocacy: deferring to clients. In fact, after the conference, a student might be even more inspired to address the problem of domestic violence by adopting a heroic attitude in relation to clients. Although Aristotle specifically defined epideictic rhetoric as a kind of discourse in which the audience isn't called upon to take action, Perelman and Olbrechts-Tyteca imagined it as *preparing* the audience to act. As they write, epideictic rhetoric "strengthens the disposition toward action," or what Burke would call attitude.[63] As I describe in the next chapter, the hospital program interrupted the impulse to act heroically by placing students into a disorienting environment in which their function was uncertain. At the hospital, students were given a limited role (listening to women's stories) and were prevented from giving advice, both of which helped them assume an attitude of deference.

3

At the Hospital | Learning to Defer to Others

At the conference described in the previous chapter, students learned to recognize the expertise of others; in the hospital program described in this chapter, students learned to assume an attitude of deference to that expertise. The hospital program ran from 1992 to 2011, the result of a joint effort between Lois Kanter and Pualani Enos of Northeastern's Domestic Violence Institute (DVI) and Dr. Barbara Herbert of the emergency department at Boston City Hospital, now known as Boston Medical Center (BMC).[1] The largest safety-net hospital and provider of trauma medicine in New England, BMC serves primarily poor and working-class patients, with more than two-thirds coming from racial and ethnic minority groups and almost one-quarter being native speakers of a language other than English.[2] The initial goal of the program was research. Students worked in small teams for a six-hour shift every other week for an academic year, interviewing women in the community about their thoughts, feelings, and experiences with domestic violence. Through these interviews, the program sought to understand the women's experiences so that better services could be provided to them.[3] By the time I began my study in the fall of 2009, the research project had collected more than two thousand testimonies.[4]

The second goal of the program was to function as a forum for "support and respect," where women could talk about their lives and beliefs without being judged or encouraged to take action as a result of what they divulged.[5] The program sought to interview as many women as possible, not just those whom the interviewer or the hospital staff suspected might be victims of domestic violence. A large proportion of women agreed to the interviews, providing a range of responses. Some discussed abuse they or someone they knew had experienced, while others discussed their ideas of it from portrayals in the media. To protect confidentiality and safety, interviewers approached only women who were alone or with small children, never women accompanied by other adults or someone who might be an abuser.[6] While the interviews were not intended as "a covert identification screen," women who disclosed current abuse during the interview were asked whether they wanted to speak with an experienced advocate about emergency shelters, abuse prevention orders, or other resources.[7]

The third goal of the program—and the goal most pertinent to my study— was to teach students to listen to women about domestic violence. After their supervisor identified potential women to approach, students would individually enter a patient's room to request an interview. After each interview, which lasted from a few minutes to more than an hour, students wrote up detailed narratives of the experience and debriefed with a supervisor about what they learned from the woman and how they could have listened better. In an article about the program, DVI faculty explain that their new students usually harbored "definite images of the ideal lawyer"—someone who employed "directive, hierarchical and individualistic methods of advocacy."[8] Inspired by this ideal, students resisted the idea that clients could be full partners in decision-making. For this reason, the DVI faculty designed the program to focus on listening, instructing students not to "share information or give advice or counsel" themselves.[9] If a woman disclosed abuse during an interview, students asked if she wanted to speak to an experienced advocate (the student's supervisor) and then ended the interview. Preventing students from advising or speaking for clients influenced the nature of their conversations. Rather than interviewing women with the goal of providing advocacy services, students interviewed them with the goal of understanding the women's points of view, an essential precursor to seeing them as experts in their own lives.

This chapter argues that the hospital program taught students to defer to the expertise of others through an embodied pedagogy that relied heavily on its physical location in an emergency department and one-on-one interactions with diverse people who were often sick and in pain. To explain how students learned to defer to others (in the sense of submitting to their judgment), I draw on another meaning of *defer*—to "delay," or "put off." I build on Linda Alcoff's idea that anyone seeking to speak for others should first carefully analyze and fight against the desire to do so, especially "if one's immediate impulse is to teach rather than listen to a less-privileged speaker."[10] Although students were eager to engage in traditional advocacy practices, the program thwarted that desire. In this location—far removed from the courtrooms, offices, and prisons in which law is ordinarily practiced—students were disoriented by the lack of formal cues indicating what they should do. Situated in this position, law students were unable to embody the role of the heroic lawyer.

In this chapter, I first discuss how the program's physical setting and rules prevented students from helping in ways traditionally associated with advocacy. I then examine how the mode of interviewing taught in the program gave students practice in two moves associated with rhetorical listening: listening across commonalities as well as differences and evaluating claims and cultural logics. This chapter is based on my observations of one of the teams at the hospital (which I shadowed from fall 2009 through spring 2010), interviews with fifteen law students (five of whom were team leaders), and analysis of the program's pedagogical materials.

Preventing Traditional Advocacy Practices

In my preliminary interviews with students in the hospital program, all but one cited a desire to advocate for less powerful people as a primary motivation for attending law school. (The primary motivation for the remaining student was to punish wrongdoers, including abusers.) These results are not surprising given the subject matter and Northeastern's reputation in public-interest law. In training sessions for the hospital program, Lois Kanter revealed to students that she had this attitude in her first fifteen years as an attorney. She identified with agents of power: she was a "gladiator lawyer," she felt like "some kind of god," she "wanted to beat any shark in the water." She explained that her motivations were good ("I was there to speak for people and wrest rights from the power structure") but that when she won domestic violence cases, her clients "were scared and mad" because Kanter didn't put their safety first. In sum, she "put a lot of people in danger." The hospital program, she said, was her way of making up for those years.

During my first interviews with students (before they had received any training), their discussions about their expectations for the program testified to the strength of the traditional model of advocacy. In those interviews, most students said that they expected their primary role would be to identify women in need of advocacy services, what Kathy called intake. Jonathan, for example, thought that he would be "an advocacy outlet, where they can tell their story to someone they can trust, who in turn is going to hand off their information to someone who can be an ever greater legal advocate for them." Similarly, Gretchen saw herself as part of a "first tier" that "greets [women who have been abused] and tries to figure out what's going on."

By preventing students from advising or speaking for clients, the hospital program clashed with their expectations. The program's location inside an emergency department served an important function: its setting did not readily allow students to embody the role of a lawyer in general or the attitude of the heroic lawyer in particular. A student entering a setting in which lawyers are expected to practice, such as a law firm or a courtroom, would have that expectation supported by the setting—for example, the conference rooms of a law firm and the counsel table in a courtroom. As the DVI faculty write, students beginning a clinical experience want to develop the skills involved in courtroom advocacy and have "vivid images of dealing with court staff, negotiating with opposing counsel and arguing before judges."[11]

Such expectations can be explained using Kenneth Burke's understanding of attitude as incipient action:

> Whatever the implications of an ATTITUDE, as a kind of incipient or future action, it must be by some means grounded in the set of the body now; and thus, though an *attitude* of kindness may be but the *preparation* for the doing of a kind act (a subsequent mode of behavior), it is already "behaving" physiologically in ways of its own (as a dog's implicit way of "conjugating the verb 'to eat'" is to begin by salivating, a bodily motion that in effect implies the future tense, "I will eat"; the present tense of the verb being bodily conjugated by eating; and "I have eaten" is also in its way a now, as the dog curls up for a comfortable, satisfied snooze).[12]

Burke might say that like the salivating dog in this amusing example, students entering a clinical education program would experience anticipation of their roles in embodied terms. From cultural depictions of the work of lawyers, law students entering a courtroom setting would be able to feel themselves standing at a counsel table while speaking on behalf of a client to a judge.

Law students in the hospital setting, where lawyers do not typically practice, neither encounter those physical props nor have models for what an attorney might do there. Rather than seeing counsel tables and a judge's bench, law students saw hospital beds and medical equipment. Rather than seeing judges, attorneys, and court staff, law students saw doctors, nurses, and social workers. As Roxanne Mountford argues, such spaces have material as well as cultural dimensions for rhetorical action. The cultural dimensions affect how people interpret the space as well as their own possibilities within it; the material dimensions inform what rhetorical practices can happen there.[13] At the hospital, a law student cannot "approach the bench" (a lawyerly act designed to speak with the judge without others hearing) because there are no benches (and, of course, no judges).

Although any hospital setting would probably be disorienting for most law students, entering the emergency department of BMC was especially so for students in 2009. Prior to a massive redesign of the campus begun in 2014, the emergency department had an unassuming, gritty entrance that was hard to find without a map. The area was not considered particularly safe. Students (and I, as an observer) were discouraged from walking alone to and from the nearby bus stops or parking garages late at night. During the first month of the program, a stabbing occurred in a waiting room just outside the office used by the students; one of the students witnessed the stabbing, and another was confined for hours in the office while police investigated. But even before they visited the emergency department for the first time, students received warning that working in a hospital poses unique risks. Fall 2009 saw a global outbreak of H1N1 flu, which eventually resulted in more than 284,000 deaths, hitting younger people especially hard.[14] Students were encouraged to be vigilant with hygiene while in the hospital and to monitor their own health.[15]

Once in the emergency department, students saw sick and injured people, and they encountered unpleasant smells from human bodies and disinfectants. Roberto commented on people vomiting in front of him and a woman "leaving a trail of blood behind her." Kathy had a particularly strong reaction to the hospital setting, which she partly attributed to her age (fifty-one), saying, "I'm at that the age where you start facing your mortality. . . . So looking around and seeing elderly people really sick and hooked up to machines for me is really anxiety causing." Other students had strong reactions to the hospital but viewed it in more positive terms and considered it exciting. Hannah, for example, thought it was "really cool" to be in the emergency department and that it was "good practice to not be in your office where you're really comfortable and to have all of these new distractions and smells and sounds, and it's a little bit chaotic."

The manual for students warned them that the setting might be intimidating because of the chaos of being in a trauma unit during emergencies, when busy medical professionals "may respond abruptly."[16] Early training for the students included a tour of the emergency department. The tour helped some students, such as Gretchen, "picture . . . the logistics of moving around" before working their first shifts. But for most students, the first shift was still intimidating. On Kim's first night, the emergency department was "pretty jammed," with "beds in the hallway [and] a ton of people in every room." She described herself and the three other students on her team as "deer in headlights" while moving through the department with their team leader to identify potential women to interview. Kelly's team, similarly disoriented, used walking around the emergency department to gather courage to approach their first patients.

By my second interview with students (after they had completed both the training and their first shifts), almost all of them understood that their primary role in the program was to learn to listen, not to screen for women in need of advocacy services. As Kathy explained, "It really didn't hit me until we were going through it that really, the goal was me . . . and my interviewing skills and my experience in talking to different kinds of people." Some framed the purpose narrowly as helping them become better interviewers. Jessica saw the benefit coming from having conducted interviews with people "lying in bed, moaning in pain, and people constantly walking by" so that other interviews later in their careers would be easy by comparison. Kelly understood the program as helping her "get the skills that we're going to need when we are practicing." For Gretchen, the program was intended to make students "better listeners" and to help them "deal with people from different cultures, different races, [and] different socio-economic [classes]." Roberto framed the educational benefit in terms of attitude, saying, "They're not trying to make you this hero that can save people through your interaction with them. You're there to listen."

Early on, most students felt uncomfortable with the prospect of bothering people in pain by asking them for an interview, especially on the topic of domestic violence. Kelly, for example, felt guilty not only because she was unable "to give them medicine . . . and . . . ease their pain" but because she was "there to annoy them" by talking about something that "isn't a topic that people jump to discuss anyway." On her first shift, Kim remembered the reluctance of one of her team members to approach women that the team leader was pointing out as potential interviewees: "Every time the team leader [said], 'You go ask her,' [she would say], 'Really? She's really old.' 'Okay, go ask her.' 'Really? She looks like she's sleeping.' 'Okay, go ask her.' 'Really? She looks really sick.'"

In an article about the program, the faculty say, "The primary obstacle for most students is simply entering the patient's room to introduce themselves and request the interview."[17] A few students reported looking for someone who wasn't "scary" or "intimidating." What that meant varied from student to student. Liz chose an older woman because she reminded her of a grandmother and seemed "harmless." Kim felt less intimidated in the pediatrics section. Roberto reported being particularly intimidated by a woman who was "angry and big" because she reminded him of his mother, saying, "I know when a woman's upset, and I know to take cover when a woman's upset. . . . I'm just wary of angry women in general."

Kathy (fifty-one) and Jonathan (twenty-nine), the two oldest students (and those with work experience involving interviewing), had the least trouble approaching patients. Jonathan, who had worked as a journalist for nine years before law school, was particularly unfazed, even from the beginning. During his first shift, another student had decided against interviewing a woman who had looked angry. After learning from a nurse that the woman was "crabby," Jonathan approached her. She twice insisted that she didn't have time for an interview because she was being moved to another room, but Jonathan convinced her to talk while she was waiting. They talked for ten minutes or so, during which time she expressed thoughtful opinions about domestic violence in the Caribbean (where she was from) and her current neighborhood in Boston. At the end, she told him that she had enjoyed the conversation. Jonathan believed that after experiencing "six and a half frustrating hours [of] nurses coming and going, doctors coming and going," the woman was glad to finally have someone "put that much value in her opinion."

As students completed their first shifts at the hospital and fully realized that they were not functioning primarily to identify women in need of services, they experienced what adult learning theorist Jack Mezirow calls a "disorienting dilemma." Experiences that challenge an "established perspective," disorienting dilemmas can result from major life events such as illness or retirement but also from everyday events such as "eye-opening" conversations, encounters with art, or engagement with cultures that are different from one's own. A disorienting dilemma can provoke a "perspective transformation," which is important to adult learning.[18] Students in the hospital program were disoriented by being prevented from assuming a role that they could imagine, one that would draw on traditional understandings of advocacy. Although students could understand their role *as students*, they faced a dilemma about another function: What was their relationship to the women they were interviewing?

For the most part, students looked for ways to see themselves as helping the women they interviewed, even if not in the way they had originally imagined.

Most thought that the women got something from the interviews themselves. At the most basic level, they thought that many women were happy to have a conversation as a distraction (what Liz described as a brief respite from pain for one of her interviewees) or just to pass the time, especially because they might wait for hours to be seen by hospital staff. Kelly, who spoke with a woman who had tried to commit suicide the night before, thought that the woman had appreciated speaking with a "neutral person" who wasn't associated with the hospital. Several thought that speaking about domestic violence might help challenge the perception that it's a topic best kept in the shadows. Some students thought that talking might help women realize that their own relationships might not be healthy. Liz spoke to one woman who had told her about leaving a violent relationship. She thought that the interview enabled the woman "to relive the story and the success of it" and therefore see herself as in control of her life. Gretchen believed that her interview with a woman who admitted her own abusive behavior allowed the woman a kind of absolution.

Many students continued to hope to identify victims through the interviews. Kathy compared the experience to television shows about emergency-room doctors who hope for accident victims so that they can practice their medical skills and help real patients at the same time. Liz had the same desire, which she said was "sort of morbid": "I want to be able to talk to someone and have them disclose to us and have us able to help them." Although she did not "want women to come in who are victims of domestic violence," she was eager to see how she would respond if they did.

When women did disclose abuse, students were trained to briefly explain the range of services available at the hospital and that these services could be provided by an experienced advocate. Students were to ask the woman's permission to introduce her to the team leader. If she agreed, the team leader would discuss with the woman her situation and options for keeping herself safe. The student's role at this point was to assist the team leader. The manual provided to students explains the role as follows: "While [our program] believes in a teamwork approach, there is a hierarchy within our teamwork model. The team consists first and foremost of the patient (who makes all decisions), then of the experienced [team leader] (who provides information, options and empowering encouragement) and finally of the [students] (who are there to assist and to learn the skills of advocacy)."[19] This explanation subverts the hierarchy of traditional advocacy, which places the professional at the top and the client at the bottom.

Students longed to be involved in this process, both to learn more and to engage in traditional advocacy practices. As Kelly explained, "I'd like to learn more about the advocacy piece. . . . I don't want to say 'I hope' because that means that somebody's got to be in that situation in order for you to come across it, but it would be nice to do a service piece to get that feeling of we're actually helping somebody." When I asked Jonathan near the end of the program about his most memorable interview, he described someone who had disclosed abuse and received services from the team leader:

> She had been abused by her roommate, her female roommate—I'm try-ing to remember the details. Basically, she got a cab down to a homeless shelter near the hospital and then was raped right after she got out of the cab. And through the course of the interview, I found out that she had been dealing with some alcohol abuse problems and was really desperate for anything to get her life back on track—anything to make things more stable. And the reason I think that the interview stands out for me— beyond just the fact that it was actually the only [service] case I ended up working on, or at least the only one I ended up working on that began from an interview that I did personally—was that because of the abuse and general neglect in her life, because she had been neglected by her mom and her brother too, she was really just completely desperate for anything. . . . Throughout [this program], you never really felt too power-ful, like you're doing that much, but in this particular situation, it was almost an empowering feeling just being able to find her a place to stay for twenty-four hours or even communicate to her that you're trying to find a place for her. Just seeing the look on her face. . . . It was only a subtle shift from desperation, and maybe there was a little bit of hope that I can find a place. . . . It was really noticeable. . . . I don't think I am ever going to forget being in the room with her that night.

Jonathan did not remember the details of the woman's story so much as the look on her face when he was trying to help. Because of his role, he had not felt "very powerful" for most of the program, but the shift in her expression was "almost empowering." I wish that I had asked Jonathan why he said "almost empower-ing," but I suspect the explanation is implied in the rest of the sentence: he tried but wasn't able to find her a place in a shelter. Immediately after telling me this story, he recalled another interview, this one memorable because of the details (the woman's abusive boyfriend had thrown a plate of spaghetti at her head) and because of his inability to help. Her boyfriend had just gotten out of jail and was trying to "force his way back into her life," and she had agreed to speak to Jonathan's team leader. But before the team leader could get back to her, the woman was gone.

Although students appreciated helping their team leaders provide services, most were clearly frustrated by their inability to do more. Several students mentioned being disappointed that they were not trained to provide services themselves. Kelly said that she felt "very restricted" in her role: "I can't really do much. If they do tell me that they need services, I have to go get somebody else." She thought she might apply to be a team leader the following year so that she could "help a person as opposed to just treat them like a research subject." The student with the most direct personal and professional experience with domestic violence, Kim, was the most frustrated. She said, "I walked in with this sense of empowerment, that I'm going to help people, and now it's just a burden to go. I don't feel like we help." But she did not quit the program, because of the "off chance that [she] could change someone's life." As she explained, "That's secretly why we're all in domestic violence work, to change one or one hundred lives. There is that chance."

Students' frustrations were part of the disorienting dilemma they faced; as Mezirow explains, such dilemmas often "contradict our own previously accepted presuppositions."[20] Students in the hospital program had equated helping with the advocacy practices of offering advice and connecting clients with services. The hospital program provided an opportunity for students to experience this disorienting dilemma by preventing them from engaging in these practices. Students faced a contradiction: How can I be helping if I'm not offering advice and connecting clients with services?

Roberto seemed the least bothered by not being able to engage in traditional advocacy and even mentioned possibly repeating the program the following year in the same capacity rather than as a team leader. Here is what he said when I asked him how he understood his role near the end of the program:

> We are just there to lend an ear to these people, regardless [of whether] they've been abused or not. . . . I still feel it's really important; I feel like we aren't directly helping people maybe, but just the fact that we're giving them someone to talk to is a benefit to these people, I think. A lot of them are already having such bad luck in their lives, and just being able to tell

your opinion with someone is a big deal. When you're not conforming to society, it's frowned upon—or even for the lower income, not being able to be a part of society because of social status or lack of money. Just being able to voice your opinion to someone who is genuinely listening to you is a big help to anyone.

Roberto had described himself in our second interview as more of a listener than a talker ("When I'm out with my friends, I like to listen, that's just my thing"). Once he understood listening as his role in the program, he adapted readily, perhaps because he already identified with it. For many other students, however, this function seemed less familiar, and the idea that *listening itself could be helpful* entailed a transformation of perspective. While a disorienting dilemma can provoke an awareness of one's own world view, developing a new perspective means also "changing these structures of habitual expectation," as Mezirow explains.[21] Next, I describe how the practice of listening helped change these expectations.

Learning to Listen Rhetorically

In the previous chapter, I analyzed how the film *Defending Our Lives* encouraged students to engage in several of the moves associated with rhetorical listening. Here, I analyze how the hospital program gave students the opportunity to engage in these moves with women who were physically present. The discomfort felt by many students at the prospect of bothering women who were sick or in pain, which I described previously, signaled an awareness of their own rhetorical agency—that is, their ability to affect others through rhetorical practices (especially speaking, listening, and body language). This awareness was sharpened as they conducted and reflected on multiple interviews over several months.

The importance of listening to the program's pedagogy is made clear by the title of an article written by the DVI faculty, "Who's Listening? Introducing Students to Client-Centered, Client-Empowering, and Multidisciplinary Problem-Solving in a Clinical Setting." The article explicitly compares listening as taught in the program to traditional approaches to legal interviewing, explaining that the program "shifts the interviewing focus from talking to listening."[22] Instead of "asking prepared questions and writing down answers," students are "initiating and facilitating a discussion."[23] Instead of "directive and controlling

methods," they use "non-directive, open-ended questioning."[24] Students can
learn to listen in this setting because they are free from the responsibilities of
representing clients. Their purpose is not to identify a client's potential legal
problem but to "[learn] about her experiences, interests and perspectives."[25]
Without knowing how to listen, the DVI faculty maintain, students can't
become good interviewers.[26] In other words, one can interview and counsel clients without necessarily listening; listening is the skill that makes *effective* interviewing and counseling possible.

Open-Ended Interviews as an Alternative to Legal Interviewing

The hospital program taught a method of interviewing that is very different
from the method typically taught in law schools, both in live-client clinics in
which students advise clients and in upper-level law school courses that focus
exclusively on client counseling or teach it as part of preparation for trial
advocacy. In the traditional method, students use what is often referred to as
the *funnel technique* to translate a client's multifaceted experience into legal
terms.

The following is an example of how a lawyer might use the funnel technique,
a series of open and closed questions designed to elicit legally relevant details.
Let's assume for the sake of argument that a lawyer is working in the emergency
department for the purpose of identifying women in need of legal services.
Because the primary legal remedy for domestic violence is the abuse prevention
order, the lawyer would have in mind the legal requirements for obtaining an
order in Massachusetts, which are that the defendant caused or attempted to
cause physical harm to the client, placed the client in fear of physical harm, or
forced the client to have sexual relations.[27] The interview might go something
like this:

> LAWYER: I'm here tonight to offer services to anyone who is being hurt by a
> partner—a husband or wife, boyfriend or girlfriend. Do you feel safe at
> home? [Closed question]
> [One possibility is that the woman, feeling targeted, will say she feels
> safe even if she doesn't. Another is that she doesn't want help and says
> she feels safe. But let's assume that she's willing to disclose and wants
> help.]
> PATIENT: No. I'm afraid of my husband.

LAWYER: Can you tell me a little more about that? [Open question]

PATIENT: He yells at me, calls me names. He yells at the kids.

LAWYER: Can you tell me about the last time something like this happened? [Open question]

PATIENT: Today. He accused me of having an affair with somebody at work, and he called me a whore.

[The lawyer is getting a picture of the relationship but hasn't heard evidence that the woman meets the legal grounds for a restraining order. She decides to ask a series of closed questions pertaining directly to the grounds.]

LAWYER: Were you afraid that he was going to hurt you? [Closed question]

PATIENT: Yes.

LAWYER: Did he hurt you? [Closed question]

PATIENT: Yes, he threw me to the floor and started kicking me. I think he broke one of my ribs.

At this point, the lawyer knows that the husband placed the woman in fear of harm, attempted to cause physical harm, and caused physical harm, all grounds for obtaining an abuse prevention order. She might explain the process of obtaining an order or offer to help the woman obtain one.

The following excerpt from one of Kathy's interviews illustrates the different approach taken in the hospital program:

> I asked her what . . . she think[s] about when she hears the words *domestic violence*. She immediately said that she had experience with it. She said that she was in a violent relationship for ten years and that he was jailed several times for abusing her. . . .
>
> I asked her about the first time that it happened. She said that it occurred three years into the relationship, after her son was born. She said that they were having an argument about some food that the baby needed, and he suddenly punched her in the face and took off. . . .
>
> I asked her if she was okay now. She said that at first after she left that men yelling bothered her, but "now I just get angry and I wouldn't tolerate it." . . . He got probation the first time he hit her but then he violated it by not going to counseling, and when he hit her again, he went to jail for six months. When he came out, she felt bad and took him back, but it started again and got worse. He threatened to kill her many times, and he even

[threatened to kill her] in front of the judge. They put him in jail for one year. When he got out that time, she thought he'd change, but it got worse, and he went back to selling drugs. . . . She said that he is [currently in prison for drug possession]. . . .

I asked her if she is concerned about what might happen when he gets out of jail. She said that he doesn't know where she is. I asked if she had a victim witness advocate to keep her apprised of what was happening with him. She said no, since she doesn't have a restraining order out on him. She said that her father will tell her if he gets out. She said if there is any trouble, she could get a [restraining order] easily, although that would make things worse. That sets him off.

Most of the students in the program had not conducted interviews as part of any other law school classes and were probably unfamiliar with the funnel technique. They were introduced to it in their orientation to the program by way of comparison. They were told that the closed interviewing techniques used by lawyers can be a problem because the lawyer is trying to fit information into fixed categories. The training provided by the hospital program was designed to help them "learn to listen in a different way," which would place students "miles ahead of peers who are ready to impose legal solutions."

As illustrated in the first example, the funnel technique uses a combination of open and closed questions to prompt the respondent to provide legally relevant information (in this case, whether the woman has the legal grounds for a restraining order). As noted by the Carnegie researchers, this combination allows students to solicit both "clients' own paths of association" and "evidence relevant to meeting the criteria of a specific legal doctrine."[28] Together, open and closed questions help the lawyer develop what's called a theory of the case, which is a legally persuasive explanation of the client's story. Although most legal questions and disputes never go to trial, attorneys develop case theories in anticipation of how a trial court would view the client's actions given legal rules. As explained in a popular trial advocacy textbook, a theory of the case "must not only establish that your client is good or worthy (or that the other side is bad or unworthy), but also that the law entitles you to relief."[29]

Motivated to develop a theory of the case, traditionally trained professionals in the legal and criminal justice system may listen only for details that fit into established categories. As legal theorist Leigh Goodmark explains, legal professionals in domestic violence cases may focus on categories such as physical violence, threats to kill, or presence of a weapon, missing stories that fall outside their expectations.[30] In the hospital program, students instead learned an approach aimed at understanding the patient's experience and world view, decentering law as a focus. Using this approach, the student followed the lead of the patient, much like an ethnographic interview. The DVI manual for students explains that the purpose of the interviews is to "help us better understand women's perspective of family violence and capture their voices."[31] Students were encouraged to begin the interview with a question such as "What are your thoughts about violence in relationships?" or "Why do you think violence happens in families or relationships?"[32] Students were instructed to listen to the response and ask a follow-up question that built on that response. They were provided with a list of topics to explore (e.g., knowledge of services for those affected by domestic violence and understandings of coping and survival strategies) along with a list of follow-up questions (e.g., "What was it like?" and "How could a person handle a problem like this?").[33]

Liz's description of one of her interviews illustrates the difference between the two ways of questioning:

> I decided I wanted to just start off broadly and see where things led. And I was trying to really listen to what she was saying and be able to react with [things] like "What makes you say that?" or "Could you explain that a little bit more?" to try to lead the conversation naturally. ...If they feel like I'm sitting there with a list of questions to ask them, I don't think they see me as being as engaged and listening. ...Whereas if I go in and just say, "Hey, I just want to talk," and I wanted to keep some general questions in the back of my mind that I could bring up if we weren't talking anymore or something. But I think there was definitely a difference.

The program allowed students to see for themselves the value of allowing a client to partially direct an interview. This experience was made possible because students were taken out of traditional roles.

Listening across Commonalities and Differences

By focusing on the law rather than human experiences, the funnel approach to interviewing ignores the notion of human difference that undergirds feminist standpoint theory—namely, that people do not necessarily share the same interpretation of events, and not all similar events have the same solution. The funnel approach assumes that the legal view matters most and that human difference is irrelevant.

The hospital program sought to teach students about the heterogeneity of experience through listening. Acknowledging heterogeneity (especially that not everyone is like *me*), however, poses new challenges. What does it take for an advocate to adopt a stance of openness to these differences? Must the advocate identify at some level with the client in order to have this stance of openness? If so, what might this kind of identification look like?

The DVI's answer to these questions, explained in the student manual, is that advocates need to find similarities with clients: "Seeing similarities between yourself and your client is of particular importance, and you do share far more characteristics, interests and experiences with your clients than you might first perceive. For example, shared characteristics might be age, race, ethnic background, coming from a big/small family, having family nearby or far away, going to school, or having particular life or career goals. Where, as is often the case, a client is older than the student, the student might see similarities between the client and her older sister, mother, or grandmother."[34]

The student manual here identifies two types of similarities: those based on shared characteristics (e.g., age, race, experiences, etc.) and those based on associations (e.g., a client who is like the student's grandmother), both of which provide opportunities for rhetorical listening. Making a connection with another person based on similarities or associations allows one to assume a stance of openness in relation to that person. As the manual puts it, forging these connections "allows you to place yourself in her shoes, and is an important first step in creating an empowering and respectful client relationship."[35]

In my interviews, students reported only a few moments of identification with patients based on shared characteristics, what Burke understands as forming the basis of identification. For Burke, identification occurs when a person shares (or believes that she shares) something in common with someone or something;[36] for some law students, identification was based on a sense of common humanity. Roberto, for example, explained that "we're all human, we all have emotions," and Liz mentioned having a "human connection" based on being physically present and talking with someone. A few of the female students identified with other women based on gender. Hannah explained that she and a woman she interviewed were "both women dealing with men," and Liz thought that talking about domestic violence "automatically builds a little bond . . . [because it is] primarily a women's issue."

Kathy, who conducted some of the longest interviews (many lasting more than an hour), was unusual: she both found something in common with women she interviewed and shared with them her sense of these commonalities. Kathy told one woman that they were the same age, that their children were the same ages, that she (like the patient) had been pregnant in her forties, and that she (like the patient) had grown children move back home. When I asked why she shared this information, she said that she listened specifically for things that they had in common, explaining, "It's a mutual exchange. It's trust. I'm asking them to trust me with their feelings and their thoughts, so I'm sharing a few personal things about myself."

A few students reported metonymic identifications, or those based on association. When forming a metonymic identification, someone recognizes associations—rather than commonalities—with another person. For example, Roberto identified with a woman not because she was like him but because she was like his mother, who had also been abused. As Krista Ratcliffe explains, listening metonymically is a tactic that provides a way of acknowledging the intersectional identities of oneself and others.[37] In the previous excerpt from the student manual, the authors might assume that students would not find obvious "shared characteristics" (age, race, or experiences) with the patients they would interview, especially since the hospital serves primarily low-income communities of color, and law students (nationally) are overwhelmingly white. A young white man from a middle-class background might not identify with an older working-class African American woman unless he is encouraged to think metonymically about the possibility of association through the multiple subject positions each of them occupies.

In a case of metonymic identification, Liz offered the following explanation for how she identified with a woman who had just fled from an abusive relationship and was being counseled by the team leader:

> She had kids who were about my age, in their early twenties, and she didn't want to tell them anything about where she was or what was going on because she didn't want them to worry about her. . . . That whole time, I just wanted to call her kids, or I wanted to say, "Call your kids; they would want to know about this." . . . Her kids were twenty-two and twenty-four or something—I'm twenty-five—and all I could see when I

looked at her, I was like, "That could be my mom." ... These are real people, and all I could think was, If this was my mother sitting in a hospital bed talking to these other women, why am I not there? . . . She didn't want them to worry. That's what she said; she said, "I don't want them to worry about me," implying that they had worried about her a lot in the past. So she didn't want them to be burdened by her. And I can see that too. My mother is like that with us too. She doesn't want us to worry.

In identifying with the woman's children, Liz first placed herself in their shoes, thinking that they would worry about her. She then refocused her attention on the woman, using her own mother to consider what the woman (rather than the children) wanted. She was able to see the woman's perspective, the foundation of a client-empowering stance, simultaneously with a perspective more similar to her own.

The most common type of metonymic identification concerned the interview context, with students placing themselves in the position of being approached by a stranger in the hospital. Usually, this identification was about feeling targeted as a possible victim of domestic violence. As Kim explained after her first shift, "I'm having a problem going up to a female, skinned knees or black eye, whatever, and saying, 'I want your opinion on domestic violence,' because my first reaction is, I'm a female. If I were in her position with a broken arm in an emergency room . . . I would feel threatened by that question."

Much more frequently, students reported feeling a lack of identification, usually based not on one category (race, class, family structure, or geography) but on multiple ones. For example, although Hannah related as a woman to her first interviewee, the differences between them seemed more pronounced. Hannah, who is white, recognized her "privilege differences" because of class and race, noting that she grew up as the youngest child of "two parents in the suburbs." In comparison, the woman she interviewed was the oldest of ten siblings from different fathers who "were very much in and out of her life, [with] a mother [who] barely paid attention to her."

Although the manual for students, along with their training, emphasizes finding commonalities, the lack of identification experienced by students could provide another place for rhetorical listening. Hannah's experience is an example of nonidentification, which Ratcliffe describes as "a place that invites people to admit that gaps exist."[38] Unlike disidentification, which involves a disavowal or rejection, nonidentification does not mean seeing the other as abject.[39] Hannah did not disavow the woman she interviewed; she did not see the woman as worthless or contemptible. Instead, she described the woman as "charismatic and confident" while still recognizing their profound differences.

For nonidentification to function as a place for rhetorical listening, the listener must be conscious of the gaps in commonality, or "the partiality of our visions," according to Ratcliffe.[40] Jonathan revealed such consciousness when explaining how he and one of his interviewees "came from different worlds." The interviewee had explained that abused women in her neighborhood had no options except to talk to other women or "smash the car windows . . . of their abuser[s] or slash the tires because they couldn't fight back." As Jonathan remarked to me, "In terms of problem solving, I don't think I would ever smash up someone's car. Well, I've never been abused either. . . .I can't stand in those shoes. I certainly don't have that experience."

Nonidentification can lead a listener to new identifications or to "revisit former identifications and disidentifications."[41] For Alexandra, nonidentification based on parenthood prompted her to revisit her initial identification based on gender. In her first interview, Alexandra initially felt connected because they were both women. But when she asked whether the woman had experienced domestic violence, the woman started offering abrupt answers, with the interview ending soon afterward. Alexandra wondered whether the presence of the woman's children in the room made it difficult for her to talk. As she explained, "I'd like to think that we as women would stick together," but not having children meant that she couldn't "even pretend to know" what the other woman's life was like.

Listening in places of nonidentification can help an advocate recognize a client's experience as different from her own, a first step toward seeing a client as an expert in her own life. Next, I explore how students began to see clients as experts in their own lives by evaluating both the content of their statements and their underlying assumptions.

Evaluating Claims and Cultural Logics regarding Domestic Violence

One of the goals of the hospital program was for students to learn about domestic violence from women in the community who had experienced or witnessed it. Hearing firsthand accounts of domestic violence gave students an understanding of the dynamics of abusive relationships as well as the structural conditions within which victims tried to keep themselves safe. As described in the previous chapter, the women in *Defending Our Lives* provided students with a good introduction to the experience of domestic violence. At the hospital, students were affected by the embodied immediacy of the disclosures. Kelly directly contrasted the experience with watching the film, saying, "Meeting people who have had that kind of a life as opposed to just reading about it or watching a movie about it— it's eye-opening to know that yes, there are people that this happens to. You know it, but you don't *know it* know it. . . . It's remote until it's not anymore."

For students, rhetorical listening offered a way to evaluate not just claims about domestic violence but also cultural logics, which Ratcliffe defines as "a belief system or shared way of reasoning within which a claim may function."[42] Listening to many women over the course of six months helped students evaluate the dominant myth, or claim, that domestic violence "doesn't affect many people."[43] In our final interviews, many of the students commented that they were shocked by the number of women they interviewed who had been abused or knew someone who had been. Jessica said that all but one of the women she interviewed had personal experience with domestic violence. Near the end of the program, Liz had interviewed so many women with experiences of domestic violence that she had come to expect (rather than be surprised by) disclosures.

Hannah extrapolated these numbers to her own life, saying, "It's not limited to certain races or socioeconomic classes. . . . It is really across the board. Which makes me think . . . If one in four women [experience domestic violence], how many women do I know have or will or are currently going through this kind of experience?" Listening to so many women helped Hannah evaluate another claim about domestic violence—namely, that it "only occurs in poor, urban areas."[44] Hannah instead surmised that domestic violence must occur across all races, classes, nationalities, and neighborhoods. But not all students made this leap. Liz, for example, said, "In my own life, I don't really [know] a lot of people who have been involved [with domestic violence], but I feel like in these neighborhoods, it's just really common."

The stories that students heard gave them new insight into the choices faced by women in abusive relationships, helping explain the cultural logics of their actions. During his first shift, Roberto interviewed a woman whose abuser had attacked her with a machete when she left the relationship. I heard about this interview not just from Roberto but from other students on his team, who were shocked by the severity of the violence. The woman's story was an implicit response to the question often asked about victims: "Why didn't she just leave?" (Answer: [1] she did leave and was attacked as a result, and [2] this man's desire to maintain control over this woman was so strong that there was no such thing as "just leaving.")

When I asked Jessica what she had learned about domestic violence during her six months in the program, she replied that she "learned that it's very hard to get out of this situation," that it can take "several tries in order to get out," and that "other factors can come into play as to why you can't get out." Kathy replied similarly, explaining that some women sometimes didn't have enough money to leave; that they sometimes had to "walk away from their lives for a while, which is so tough"; or that the only shelters available couldn't take their children.

Students learned the range of things that victims do in response to violence, including strategies they use to keep themselves safe. The women left, going to stay with friends or family or in shelters; they returned for all sorts of reasons, including because the abuser promised he'd change or because she had nowhere else to go; they changed their own behavior, hoping to minimize the frequency and severity of attacks; they called the police; they got restraining orders; they fought back; they sought support from friends and family; they screamed for help. Hearing about these strategies helped law students see those in abusive relationships as not just passive victims, as they are commonly portrayed in popular and legal discourses. Women in abusive relationships are often characterized as incapable of leaving or helping themselves, as being totally under someone else's control, and as being pathologically destined to be with an abuser. Law students in this program described the women they interviewed as strong, resilient, and knowledgeable—a far cry from these stereotypes.

Students were also exposed to the unattractive effects of domestic violence. The DVI manual for students explains that while those working with victims might "expect [victims] to welcome assistance, to be cooperative and grateful for the services offered, and to look optimistically toward a better future," the reality is often quite different. The manual emphasizes instead that "violence and degradation only rarely ennoble the object of abuse."[45] A service case gave Gretchen a window into these effects. Her team was working with a woman who had decided to leave her abuser and needed space in a shelter. While the team leader and a couple of students worked with the woman to find her a bed, Gretchen and others students attended to her three-year-old child. She overheard the conversation between the woman and the people who ran the shelter: "The shelter called her, and they were asking her what she needed for her son and what kind of food they liked. [They were] going to go the supermarket that night before they got there and get things for them. [She] was like, 'Oh no, I don't like that; no, I don't really like that; yeah; no; no, actually, could you get this; [blah, blah, blah]' instead of 'Oh my God, thank you so much, that is above and beyond'—that kind of thing. It was just . . . not how I would have responded in the same situation." On reflection, Gretchen thought of the woman's response in the context of her situation, explaining that "she takes what she can get because she lives a tough life, and if someone is going to get groceries for her, awesome— she'll take it with two hands because she needs to."

Gretchen's team leader remembered that a number of students on the team had issues with the same client as a parent. As the students played with the child, the team leader noticed that he seemed exhausted and that "he slammed his head down on the floor in frustration or being tired or whatever." He then "started to cry, and his mom just didn't make any move to go to him or comfort him and just kind of watched." Several students thought that she was being neglectful. The team leader encouraged them to examine the reasons for the woman's behavior:

> If we look at what happened to her earlier that day, her life was threatened for the first time in a very real way by her boyfriend, who had been controlling her, and then finally that day he said, "If you call the police, I will kill you." We know that domestic violence makes it hard to be the parent you want to be, and if you honestly think that someone is going to murder you, I can't imagine that I would be the most attentive mom either. . . . It is hard to watch someone not be a good parent, especially when the kid is one of those helpless people along with his mom and she's not taking care of him. That's hard to see, but there are reasons why that happens.

Both Gretchen and the team leader placed themselves into the woman's situation as a way of trying to understand the logic of her actions.

Several students commented explicitly on the value of this kind of understanding. Roberto recounted an interview with a woman who placed blame for violence on the victims. Although Roberto didn't agree with her, he enjoyed hearing her perspective, calling it "a chance to see more of the world because everyone has their section of the world they see, and you just put it all together." Jessica agreed, saying, "I think all the information helps, just because you can understand why people do the things that they do. Even if they're not logical to you, it always helps to get an understanding of why it happens." For Kathy, understanding someone else's point of view was as much about her as it was about the other person. When I asked her what she'd gotten most out of the program, she said, "Self-awareness," explaining that she learned how to understand "how I was feeling and what I was thinking and trying not to judge and put my own values. . . .We all learn this as you grow up . . . that your reaction to something could be very different than someone else['s] based on what their life has been like."

Significantly, many of the students reported a new understanding of the limits of legal responses to domestic violence. Jonathan was surprised to hear so many accounts of police responding nonchalantly to domestic violence calls, "with the police telling them to just patch things up and, you know, keep it quiet, and . . . 'Don't be hitting her,' and 'Don't be aggravating him.'" Gretchen had a more fundamental shift in thinking. She explained that she used to see domestic violence as a "cut-and-dried criminal law–enforcement problem," meaning that "if someone beats you up and you want him to stop . . . then you call the police and they arrest [him] and you file charges." However, by the end of the program, she saw domestic violence as more of a "sociological problem." Whereas arrests and criminal prosecutions would make sense for some people, Gretchen explained that for others, this kind of response "either increases the level of danger to them or it's just not actually going to do anything."

Kathy had a similar revelation after reflecting on how little the law or the criminal justice system came up in her interviews:

> The law and the court process . . . was so ancillary. It really wasn't the focus of any discussion. It was sort of there, but it wasn't ever the reason or the solution to people getting better, getting help, getting out. It was there because I would ask. Even with my interviews, we'd have really deep questions, and no one ever brought up "Oh, I called the cops" or "I went to court." . . . I didn't actually realize it until you and I are talking about it, but any information that I ever got about whether they got restraining orders or whether they called the cops to their house [or] whether the perpetrator went to jail were things I asked. And they said, "Oh, yeah" . . . but it wasn't the thing that they thought about because the law is not going to be there 95 percent of the time that they are dealing with this.

Kathy had this revelation because she had not made legal solutions the focus of her interviews, as she would have in a traditional legal interview using the funnel technique. Liz reflected on this disconnect in relation to legal education. Because "a lot of [domestic violence advocacy] has nothing do with legal issues," she said, law school education "doesn't really match up to the type of training it necessarily takes to do [this work.]"

This shift in understanding was probably the most striking pattern in my interviews with students. I believe it accounts for the faith the DVI faculty put in the hospital program to prepare students for client-empowering advocacy. Many of these students went on to work as interns for the DVI or enrolled in the court clinic program (described in the next chapter). Compared to those who had not had the hospital experience, these students were more likely to see clients as partners, to view legal intervention as only one option among many, and to understand and respect clients' decisions, no matter what they were.[46] Far away from courtrooms and law offices, the hospital program prevented students from too quickly assuming a role they thought they understood, deferring traditional acts of advocacy until they had a better understanding of domestic violence. This deferral gave students time to develop skills in rhetorical listening as well as an appreciation for listening to clients. By the time they entered what the faculty describe as "the frequently hierarchical, disempowering atmosphere of the legal system,"[47] these students had decentered law in their own imaginations, making it possible for them to resist the heroic attitude and embrace an attitude of deference toward their clients.

4

At the Courthouse | Learning to Support the Rhetorical Work of Others

At the conference described in chapter 2, students learned about the complex personal, social, and cultural contexts of domestic violence, including how those contexts affect a person's choices and decision-making. They learned that those abused by intimate partners have an expertise in their own lives that can never be replaced by an advocate, no matter how well intentioned. In the hospital program described in the previous chapter, students heard directly from women about domestic violence in a setting that prevented the students from engaging in traditional acts of advocacy. By listening rhetorically to these women, students developed strategies for working with clients that differed substantially from the methods usually taught in law schools. Students who subsequently entered the court program described in this chapter (including four of the five students I follow) built on these strategies in their encounters with clients.

In the court program, students served as advocates for clients who came to Boston Municipal Court seeking abuse prevention orders. These orders—also called personal protection orders, no contact orders, and restraining orders—are the primary means by which victims in the US use the legal system to protect themselves against partner violence. Abuse prevention orders are available in all fifty states, although their provisions vary.[1] Through the 1978 Abuse Prevention Act, individuals in Massachusetts can appear before a judge and obtain an abuse prevention order without an attorney or court fees.[2] Some, like Jennifer Martel, receive emergency orders through the police when the courts are closed, although they must appear in court the next business day if they want to have an order extended.

According to judicial guidelines, anyone applying for an order may be assisted by an advocate, who might be a law student, a volunteer from an advocacy group, or a friend or family member. In some courthouses, groups specializing in domestic violence (such as the Domestic Violence Institute [DVI]) have established a presence so that victims have access to trained advocates whose only interest is serving the client.[3] Individuals who receive emergency orders outside of regular court hours, such as Martel, might be contacted by an advocate serving in this capacity. (In her case, Martel was called by a victim witness advocate, an employee of the district attorney's office, the morning after she received an emergency order. But she did not speak with a domestic violence specialist.[4]) According to the guidelines, courts must provide space for advocates to work with plaintiffs and must allow advocates to help plaintiffs with the filing process, including "aid[ing] and support[ing] a party during the hearing to the extent that the party wishes it and the court deems it helpful."[5] Judges vary in the degree to which they expect advocates to take an active role in hearings.

Like students at the hospital, students in the court program learned to cultivate an attitude of deference partly because they were constrained in their roles, both by institutional norms, as some judges expected advocates to say little, and by the ideological focus of the program on client empowerment. For these reasons, students were largely prevented from doing what attorneys usually do: speak for their clients.[6] Instead, they learned to support their clients' rhetorical work, which is itself an act of rhetoric, as Jeff Grabill notes. This support requires students to pay attention to "the mundane, the technical, the routine" as a way to "build capacity with others to act effectively."[7] Law students in the court program built this capacity through a range of practices. In many cases, this support taught clients themselves to be more effective rhetors; thus rhetorical education was occurring on multiple levels.

While assuming an attitude of deference might lead an advocate to support the rhetorical work of clients rather than speaking for them, performing the practices that constitute this support in turn helped students learn this attitude. In other words, students learned deference by performing deference. By undertaking these practices, students developed *mētis*—an embodied intelligence essential to understanding not only *how* to perform them but whether and when to do so. These performances, like all acts of rhetoric, were embodied experiences. They were acts of individuals whose bodies informed not only their world views but sometimes also the form of rhetorical practice (e.g., body language and speech).

I begin this chapter by considering how the embodied experiences of advocates formed the basis for identifications and nonidentifications with their clients. Identifications and nonidentifications—especially those based on race and class—both emerged from and contributed to an approach to clients as individuals and advocacy practices as contextual. I then turn to the situated pedagogy of the court clinic program. Through this pedagogy, steeped in feminist explanations of domestic violence, students developed *mētis* through action and supervised learning by doing. Finally, I describe how advocates supported their clients (and in many cases, instructed them) in rhetorical work, including deliberating about what to do, establishing a presence in the courtroom, and creating a credible *ethos*. Law students and clients formed a partnership so that the work of advocacy didn't belong solely to the person occupying the position of advocate or to any single actor. In this context, then, advocacy and its pedagogy is what Grabill might call "coordinated and distributed" rather than individually held and practiced.[8]

Identities, Identifications, and Advocacy Practices

In contrast to speaking primarily for oneself, seeking to speak for, speak with, or enable the rhetorical practices of another means that the opportunities for identification, nonidentification, and disidentification are magnified. In what follows, I attempt to lay out how identities mattered to both the advocates in my study and their clients and how identification and nonidentification mattered to practices of advocacy by influencing what clients disclosed, whether advocates attempted to understand their clients' ways of seeing the world (their cultural logics), and the extent to which advocates deferred to their clients' expertise.

The law students in this program worked at the Roxbury and Dorchester divisions of the Boston Municipal Court, which serve a racially, ethnically, and linguistically diverse, primarily low-income population. The population across both neighborhoods from 2007 to 2011 was about 50 percent black or African American, 10–20 percent white, and 3–10 percent Asian, with a quarter to a third of people from all races identifying as Hispanic or Latino. A quarter to a third were foreign born—with most immigrants coming from the Caribbean islands, Cape Verde, or Vietnam—and nearly half spoke a language other than English. A quarter to a third of households received food stamps, and more than half were living in poverty. By way of comparison, the population from the Back Bay area of Boston—which is called by the City of Boston "one of America's most desirable neighborhoods" and whose boundaries begin less than a half mile from those of Roxbury—was approximately 81 percent white, nearly 4 percent black or African American, and about 8 percent Asian, with around 6 percent of people from all races identifying as Hispanic or Latino. More than 75 percent were born in the US and spoke English only, and only about 3 percent were unemployed. Very few households (about 3 percent) received food stamps, and roughly 13 percent were living in poverty.[9]

When members of the Roxbury and Dorchester neighborhoods come before the court, their identities matter to how they understand (and value) the legal and criminal justice systems and what relief they seek. I borrow from critical race theorist Kimberlé Crenshaw the idea that identities are intersectional rather than monolithic—that is, that membership in any single group (marked by race, class, gender, nationality, etc.) doesn't wholly determine one's identity but operates in conjunction with membership in other groups. Because of the disproportionate incidence of poverty among people of color, as well as employment and housing practices that discriminate against them, women of color experience domestic violence in qualitatively different ways than their racially privileged counterparts. Immigrant status can also differentiate one's experience, as immigrant women may deal with fears of deportation, limited access to resources, and language and cultural barriers that further isolate them.[10]

Their identities also impact how they are treated by court personnel, especially judges. At the time this study was conducted, 10.5 percent of Massachusetts state court judges identified as a racial ethnic minority, and 34.2 percent were women.[11] Only a few years after the Massachusetts Abuse Prevention Act was signed into law, a study revealed widespread noncompliance, with gender- and race-based discrimination on the part of judges being one of the top complaints.[12] In one case, a judge known to "routinely harass women" who petitioned for restraining orders issued an order but "[chastised the woman] for 'doing a terrible disservice to the taxpayers' by taking up the court's time when it 'has a lot more serious matters to contend with.'"[13] The judge also told her that she did not need police protection. The woman, Pamela Nigro Dunn, was murdered by her husband in 1986.

According to sociologist James Ptacek, Dunn's murder spurred feminist organizing that led to increased surveillance of judges.[14] Several years after the murder, Ptacek conducted an ethnography of how Massachusetts judges treated women who had applied for abuse prevention orders. In his study (conducted from 1992 to 1994), Ptacek examined case files, observed hearings, and interviewed both judges and women seeking orders in Boston Municipal Court, including one of the court divisions (Dorchester) where the advocates in my study worked. Ptacek argues that judges sometimes empowered women (through such actions as informing women about their legal options or encouraging them to talk about their fears), but sometimes instead reinforced the abusers' power by making harsh or racist remarks or saying that the woman caused the abuse.[15] He also noticed that judges tended to ignore women's requests for child support or other monetary relief, surmising that the women's "class and racial characteristics seem to mark them as untrustworthy and as wasting the court's time with their concern[s] for material relief."[16]

Ptacek's study illustrates what feminist legal theorist Carol Smart has argued about law: while it is not a single unified entity, it routinely "resists and disqualifies alternative accounts of social reality," including accounts based on the experiences of women.[17] Although law isn't unified, it has systemic features that tend to privilege particular groups at the expense of others. According to Smart, law tends to privilege its own ways of knowing above others, including everyday experiences, in its efforts to define the "truth" of events.[18] Rather than applying equally and blindly to everyone, law's definitions, assumptions, policies, and procedures presume a very specifically situated person. This ideal legal subject, whom feminist legal theorist Ngaire Naffine calls "the man of law," is an educated, middle-class man who embodies a particular kind of masculinity that is competitive, aggressive, and individualistic.[19] As critical race theorists have argued, the man of law is also white.[20]

The identities of advocates also matter to how they are perceived at the court. Although Ptacek didn't focus on or interview advocates in his study, he argues that advocates, mostly female, play a gendered role within the institution of the court, along with the mostly female clerical staff of the courthouse, because they are perceived to humanize "the bureaucracy, providing compassion and support."[21] All the advocates who took part in my study were women, although other advocates in the program were men. All advocates were also in their second or third years of law school. The following brief biographies provide a glimpse of other aspects of their identities:

- ✦ Chloe, twenty-five, identified as African American and was raised as a Jehovah's Witness. Chloe had participated in the hospital program and had worked subsequently as a domestic violence advocate for the same hospital. Chloe came to law school and Northeastern University School of Law specifically to study domestic violence advocacy. She was motivated to pursue the work because many women in her family, including her mother and grandmother, had experienced physical, emotional, or sexual abuse.

+ Hannah, twenty-seven, identified as white and Jewish. She had participated the previous year in the hospital program and took part in my study of that program. After graduating from college, she had worked as a human rights accompanier in Central America and did intake for a legal aid office. She was motivated to attend law school and become involved with the DVI because of a desire to help people affected by violence. During law school, she worked on the US-Mexico border with two different immigrant advocacy groups.

+ Helen, twenty-six, identified as Asian American and not religious. Helen had participated in the hospital program as both an interviewer and a team leader (when she took part in my study of that program). Helen decided to attend law school because of her interest in women's rights and domestic violence and chose Northeastern because of the DVI. During law school, she worked for the family and probate court and with a domestic violence advocacy center.

+ Samantha, twenty-six, identified as African American, a child of immigrants from the Caribbean, and Christian. She grew up in the neighborhood served by the court where she worked. Unlike the other four advocates, she did not participate in the hospital program. Before law school, she worked for several years in a district attorney's office, sometimes assisting victim witness advocates. She was motivated to attend law school by the desire to "give people a voice." She took part in the court clinic program partly because of her own experience in a long-term emotionally abusive relationship with a suicidal and violent man.

+ Talia, twenty-three, identified as white, of Middle Eastern descent, and not religious. Like Chloe, Talia had participated in the hospital program the previous year and then had worked the following summer as a domestic violence advocate for the same hospital. As an undergraduate student, Talia had completed a medical internship in domestic violence in a hospital emergency department in New York. After graduating from college, she conducted research in the Middle East on women's access to health care. Talia chose Northeastern University School of Law because of the DVI and its public interest focus.

Advocates' racial identities informed how they understood their roles in relation to clients and the legal and criminal justice systems, including beliefs about how institutions work with variously situated people. In her work at the court, Chloe found race the most obvious line of identification and nonidentification:

> I appreciate that we're in an area that's predominantly African American, people of color, and low income....It was interesting and kind of depressing to be a woman of color and to see mainly black people in trouble with the law, but the good side was that I felt being an advocate helping out people who look like me was very empowering for me. . . .Mainly the DAs [district attorneys] are white. A lot of probation officers are white. The clerks are white. The judges—I can only think of two black judges— the rest of them are white. And you're seeing arraignments, just sitting in the sessions and looking at the fishbowl of all the people who were arrested, seeing people who look like you. It can be depressing. But to see people who have an authoritative or professional role in the court [who look] like you is very empowering. Something as simple as seeing that the security are African American, the fact that the head of the clerk's office is a black man, and there's one assistant DA that's black. I feel like it's very empowering. The fact that there are two judges—even though those two judges I might not be particularly fond of—they're black, so that's empowering.

Chloe was experiencing what Patricia J. Williams calls "feelings of exaggerated visibility and invisibility [that] are the product of . . . not being part of the larger cultural picture."[22] For Chloe, race connected her to most of the people doing business with the court and a handful of those in positions of power, but race contributed to a sense of nonidentification with most of the people in power. Significantly, she saw her race as a bridge that could help her connect her clients with the institution, as she was both African American and a member of the court staff.

While Chloe focused on the positive effects of this empowerment for herself as a woman of color, Hannah found that identifying with those in power could make it more difficult to identify with clients, saying, "We wear a suit to court twice a week, and . . . all sorts of people come up to me and ask me all these different questions and whether or not I can help them. Just wearing a suit makes you feel like hot shit because you look so different than the people who are coming into Dorchester Court. Not only do you not look like them, but you look like the people that hold all of the cards in the courtroom." Hannah focuses here on a symbol of class—the suit, which advocates were required to wear to court—but at another point, she focuses on the intersection of race and class, calling herself "a white girl in a suit." Importantly, Hannah thought that race, class, and education combined to create a dangerous sense of privilege: "I think people get off on this sense that they are part of this elite club. And sadly, you are part of this elite club. . . .So it's not intuitive to have a [client-empowering] practice. And you do know a lot. You know a lot more than the clients about the law. But you don't know a lot more about your client."

Thus advocates' identities also informed to what extent (and along what lines) they identified with their clients and vice versa. These identifications (as well as nonidentifications) were negotiated at every moment and were based on multiple facets of identity rather than on single ones, such as gender or race. Samantha, for example, said that these identifications are always "a combination. Even for myself, as a female of color in law school, getting a [client who is a] female of color who may not be in law school, who may not be working, who may feel intimidated and not want to talk to me, or thinks I'm looking down at her or judging her—so it doesn't have to be just race. It could be that polar opposite. [That client may be thinking,] 'I didn't go to college; I hope this girl doesn't think I'm a bad person or an unfit person.'" Other lines of identification and nonidentification (besides gender, race, class, and level of education) mentioned by students included the following:

- *Age.* Helen had difficulty connecting with a client who was "a lot older" and felt that her supervisor was better able to serve the client because they were closer in age. Samantha remarked about one client, "This girl is my age. This could very well be me. Could I handle all of this by myself while also working a full-time job? Probably not." For Chloe, her most difficult clients were the ones closest to her age because she believed that age conveyed a false sense of similarity between herself and the client.
- *Neighborhood.* Growing up in the neighborhood served by one of the courts where she worked, Samantha would sometimes see people she knew from high school coming in for orders: "It's probably weirder for me than it is for other people because I grew up around here—being in court and seeing people that I know. It's hard for me because I'm like, 'Does anybody know? Have you spoken to anybody else?' They feel comfort in talking to me, but I don't want them to feel shame in talking to me. Just because I know you, I'm not thinking less of you."

+ *Personal experiences with abuse.* As someone who had had difficulty extricating herself from an emotionally abusive relationship, Samantha felt that she understood when "another person may not be able to come forward or not be able speak on it." For Chloe, talking with women about abuse made her think about the women in her own family; this connection was a "safety blanket in some way."

These identifications and nonidentifications were not just about whether advocates connected with their clients; they influenced advocacy practices. First, they could influence how much clients disclosed. As critical race theorist Gerald P. López argues, clients of color working with white lawyers may wonder how much to reveal about themselves, how much to trust the lawyers' intentions, and how to evaluate the lawyers' advice.[23] Hannah thought that such caution made sense, saying, "Who am I? I'm some random white girl who's wearing a suit asking incredibly personal questions. And she didn't even ask for my services." Conversely, Chloe imagined that her clients of color felt somewhat more comfortable with her because she was African American, saying that commonalities "can build some trust with clients. . . . Sometimes it can go a long way if there's someone who looks like you a little bit or is from the same neighborhood as you and can understand where you're coming from a little bit, [especially] if you're living in a neighborhood that's filled with poverty, racism, [and] police brutality." Both Hannah and Chloe not only recognized race as an important line of identification but exhibited awareness of how race influenced their clients' experiences with the law, thus giving lie to the law's purported colorblindness.

Second, identifications and nonidentifications also influenced how the advocates understood their clients' cultural logics, the belief systems that underpin claims. Some of the advocates imagined what they would do in a similar situation while trying to account for their client's particular position. Talia, who had a client whose abuser worked as a cleaner in her apartment building and had keys to all the apartments, said that she too "would be concerned. I wouldn't want him cleaning my building." But for a client who was seeking an abuse prevention order against her sister, Talia couldn't "imagine my sister saying these things to me. It was really hard to relate to." To understand her client's point of view, Talia tried "to see it as not her sister because it didn't seem like they had any sister relationship—what I think of as normal at all." Other advocates also compared clients' situations to their own family relationships. In order to make sense of one client's situation, Chloe thought of her own mother: "My mom was a victim of abuse, and she's a great mother, and I think her feeling was that she wanted to keep her family together. So maybe that's why this girl was the same way."

Third, identifications and nonidentifications affected how much an advocate felt she could defer to her client's expertise. Both Talia and Chloe, for example, felt that identifying too much with a client made deferring to the client's expertise more difficult. Chloe said, "The hardest ones were when they were my age. . . .I would immediately think about the women in my family. . . .But at the same time, I had to recognize that their stories are completely different, and the struggles that they went through are not the same exactly as what my mom or I or my grandmother went through." Chloe here recognized what Burke calls the ambiguities of substance at the heart of identification, being "both joined and separate, at once a distinct substance and consubstantial with another."[24] Recognizing the client as consubstantial but not identical was essential for being open to her particular needs.

Talia thought that the more she identified with a client across similarities, the more she wanted to tell her what to do. She said, "You feel like you know their situation more because it's more like me. This is what I would do in this situation. We're so similar, so maybe this is best for [the client], but really it's probably not best for them. I think it is hard to stick to the client-empowerment model in those situations." In one particular case, she identified a lot with a client with similar interests (the client was going into the Peace Corps and was also considering law school). The client did not want to testify in the criminal case against her abuser. As Talia remembered, "I found myself agreeing with her too much on not testifying and wanting to move on with her life, because I felt like that's how I would want to be if I were leaving for Morocco in three months and out of this nine-year terror, this relationship. I would be like, I want to go and not think about this guy ever. . . .I was worried that I was pressuring her too much into not complying with the criminal case." Both Chloe and Talia were engaged in rhetorical listening, searching for differences with their clients as a way of recognizing and doing justice to their particular circumstances. In their cases, searching for differences led to opportunities for increased rather than diminished understanding, which Krista Ratcliffe sees as essential for ethical cross-cultural conduct.

For the advocates in this study, recognizing identity as intersectional meant seeing clients as both unique (in that no one else occupied that same subject position) and susceptible to common forms of subjugation or privilege based on social categories such as race, gender, class, sexual orientation, nationality, or ability. They learned to recognize identity as intersectional through a situated pedagogy, to which I now turn.

Situated Pedagogy

The DVI court clinic program is an academic course offered two to three times a year in twelve-week terms. It began in the early 1990s, when an associate justice of the Dorchester court invited the DVI, which had been offering legal services to women in community-based settings, to relocate to the court.[25] The clinic I studied (in 2010–11) was cotaught and supervised by Lois Kanter and a licensed attorney. During the first week of the term, students participated in twenty-five hours of intensive training to prepare them for their work at the court. Students read and discussed feminist theories of violence against women, explanations of the client-empowerment approach to advocacy, and procedures for helping clients with legal and nonlegal needs. They also engaged in role-playing exercises for abuse prevention order hearings. Most of this training took place in law school classrooms, but the students also made brief visits to the courts. After the initial training, students began working at the court for one and a half days per week. They attended class on campus once a week to discuss their collective experiences and readings and met weekly with Kanter and the other attorney for individual supervision. I sat in on the initial training, accompanied advocates on their first trip to one of the courts, and interviewed each advocate twice over three months. Although I observed abuse prevention order hearings at both courts, I did not observe hearings in which these particular advocates participated in order to help preserve the attorney-client privilege that applied to their work.

In what follows, I explain three important elements of the situated pedagogy of the clinic program—feminist-based client empowerment, embodied action, and supervised learning by doing—through a particularly memorable story told by Chloe. In broad strokes, the story went like this: Chloe's client had been assaulted by her boyfriend, who was subsequently arrested. Because of the boyfriend's violence, the client had been told by a social worker that she would lose custody of her children unless she got an abuse prevention order against the boyfriend. Although the client had not wanted the order, she agreed. During the hearing, her boyfriend's bail was revoked. When the judge announced that the boyfriend would remain in custody, the client fell to the floor and started crying. Chloe, who agreed with the decision even though it wasn't what her client wanted, felt torn. She recalled,

> When she started crying in the corner, [my supervisor] said to me in my ear, "Empathy, empathy, empathy." At that point, I was like, I don't know what to do right now. The DA's there, the victim witness advocate is right there next to me, telling me to leave her alone. [My supervisor] is like, "Get her, get her." I just knelt down and let her cry. And [my supervisor] was saying, "Tell her it's not her fault. He's not staying in jail because of her." I basically had to make her feel better and let her know that "I'm sorry your boyfriend is still in jail. It's not your fault. He can come out eventually." It was really weird to do that. That's pretty much what I was saying to her, which is not what I was hoping to say. In my mind, I was like, thank God his bail was revoked.

Chloe had seconds to respond to this complex situation. Although the initial training had not completely prepared her for such a moment, the supervisor was physically at her side, telling her how to embody client-empowering advocacy. The supervisor directed Chloe's physical response ("Get her, get her") and her verbal response ("Tell her it's not her fault"). I return to this example in a discussion of each of the elements of the program's pedagogy in the following sections.

Feminist-Based Client Empowerment

The DVI court clinic was overtly committed to a feminist, gender-based theory of domestic violence that attempted to situate clients within larger structural frameworks. Although legal educators originally had high hopes that clinical experiences would automatically engender critical perspectives to students through what López describes as "the messiness of living and lawyering," this did not turn out to be the case.[26] Instead, students learn from any clinical experience the implicit and explicit theoretical foundations of that particular experience.

The DVI's feminist commitment was reflected in a training manual provided to advocates, which was discussed in the initial training and in weekly classes and individual supervision sessions. In the manual, Kanter provides a bird's-eye view of feminist theories of domestic violence from the 1960s to the present, discusses their practical limitations, and addresses critiques, particularly from so-called family violence researchers who maintain that women and men engage equally in violent acts in intimate relationships. Kanter justifies her discussion of the program's theoretical grounding in practical terms. Drawing explicitly on intersectional theory, for example, she discusses how identity affects not only a person's experience of abuse but also the relationship between advocate and client. Most significantly, Kanter argues that a feminist, gender-based theory will explain most of the cases that students would see, providing an alternative explanation to commonsense understandings of victim behaviors. Victims, she explains, may engage in behaviors that seem counterintuitive, such as not seeking help, minimizing abuse, returning to abusers, or refusing to participate in criminal prosecution. Someone uninformed about feminist explanations of these behaviors might take them to mean that the victim is not in real danger. Feminist theory, Kanter argues, can help advocates and others (such as judges) place these behaviors into their respective social and cultural contexts and make judgments that support rather than endanger victims.[27]

Chloe's client exhibited some of this counterintuitive behavior. She did not want to participate in the criminal proceedings against her boyfriend, and she wanted him to be able to come home with her. A feminist lens attentive to issues related to intersectional identity can provide several possible explanations for her unwillingness to cooperate with the prosecutor: as a woman in a relationship with a man who wanted power and control, she might have been afraid of retribution from him; as a woman of color, she might not have wanted to be complicit in the incarceration of men of color; as a woman living in poverty, she might have been concerned about economic implications if he were imprisoned and unable to work. A feminist lens can also provide several possible explanations for the client's desire for the boyfriend to make bail: she might have been concerned about what he would do when he was released (blaming her even if she didn't participate in the criminal prosecution), she might have believed her boyfriend's promises to change, or she might have wanted to remain with the boyfriend but without the abuse.

Chloe's initial reaction to her client's desires and behavior was counter to these understandings, hence her hesitation about what to do or say. While Chloe's client was not actively making a decision in the moment described in her story, Chloe's choices about how to react to her client would convey judgment about her choice to remain with the boyfriend. Her supervisor's guidance in this moment of hesitation displayed a commitment to client empowerment. Her initial admonition ("Empathy, empathy, empathy") implored Chloe to place herself in her client's position to understand her situation but not to tell her what to do. Her later advice ("Tell her it's not her fault") encouraged Chloe to acknowledge the woman's structural position (she hadn't come willingly to the court to get an abuse prevention order, and even if she had, she was not the one who had denied him bail) and provide some psychological support against the guilt she might feel or the blame that the boyfriend might eventually lay on her.

As discussed in chapter 1, client empowerment runs counter to traditional models of legal advocacy. These traditional models pulled at the advocates, as Hannah explained:

> Intuitively, you want to tell them what to do. You think that you are a hotshot because you're wearing a suit and you sit in front of the bar and you have this body of knowledge and you are far more educated than most of your clients and you have this special key to the justice system or something. I think you have to really cultivate a client-empowerment mentality in yourself. It's not automatic at all. You have to really check yourself, check your ego, and remind yourself that it's not about you and what you think is best.

Hannah's understanding of privilege was connected not just to educational differences but to the physical location in the courtroom ("in front of the bar," which is where attorneys sit) and markers of class ("wearing a suit"). The experience of wearing a suit and being allowed in areas of the courtroom that are forbidden to the general public is part of the socialization into the law as a profession and thus carries with it some of the associations of that power ("you want to tell them what to do"). Next, I discuss the importance of the court setting to how students learned the embodied action of client-empowering advocacy.

Embodied Action

The court setting, where students spent the bulk of their time, was crucial to their learning because there they embodied a role, stepping into a system with both regularities and uncertainties and taking actions that had important material consequences for their clients. Thinking of the court as both a place and a space helps underscore its importance in students' learning. As philosopher Michel de Certeau explains, place is a geometric or physical property that "excludes the possibility of two things being in the same location."[28] Places have a certain stability; the municipal courts are physical locations, buildings separate from those around them and specifically designated for legal proceedings. Their courtrooms are permanently arranged with judges' benches, tables for clerks and attorneys, custody boxes, gallery seating, and insignia of power (e.g., state seals, flags, and portraits). A space, on the other hand, is "composed of intersections of mobile elements. . . .[A space is] actuated by the ensemble of movements deployed within it. . . .In short, *space is a practiced place.*"[29] A court is transformed into a space by the actions of people (lawyers, judges, clerks, bailiffs, security guards, probation officers, advocates, plaintiffs, defendants, observers, and others) and texts (complaints, orders, motions, oral arguments, statements, etc.). The practices of people and other actors make spaces inherently unstable. Because of this instability, outcomes are never certain.

As both a place and a space, then, the court is a seat of relatively stable institutional power and a location where power is not held by a single entity or person, even the judge. Rather, as philosopher Michel Foucault explains, "power is exercised from innumerable points, in the interplay of nonegalitarian and mobile relations."[30] I do not mean to downplay the institutional force ready to back up judges' words; however, a number of factors influence judges' decisions, including the actions of advocates and their clients. Perhaps more important, the court is not limited to the court*room*, and judicial actions are not the only actions in the court. Advocates stressed to me that their most important work was done outside of hearings, either preparing clients for them or discussing other matters, such as how to stay safe from an abuser or how to obtain new housing. In fact, most advocates said that legal counseling was a relatively small part of their job.

What students developed at the court was *mētis*. In spaces where power is distributed, such as the court, *mētis* "constantly restores the unexpected pertinence of time," as de Certeau explains.[31] Unlike the romanticized idea of lawyers operating in comfortable (often lavish) offices with plenty of time and resources, the advocates in this program usually consulted with clients on hard benches in public spaces in the courthouse. Their clients had often experienced recent trauma and sometimes were accompanied or followed by their abusers. Advocates approached clients uninvited and had to quickly establish rapport and find a safe space for consultation. They were usually under a deadline to get paper work completed before the next session, and the hearings themselves were fast, often lasting only a few minutes, giving the client and advocate very little time to understand and react to what a judge had ordered. Although the advocate's role was not a typical lawyering role, the constraints of the setting are very typical for lawyers working with subordinated people. As López explains, these lawyers "must make do in circumstances many others would find inadequate to the task of good lawyering."[32]

The type of intelligence required for such situations is not just cognitive. This kind of intelligence cannot be separated from the body because, as Debra Hawhee puts it, "thought does not just happen within the body, it happens as the body."[33] In her study of ancient Greek rhetorical education and athletic training, Hawhee argues that students developed *mētis* in both kinds of education, which often occurred alongside each other. Although these two disciplines are not taught together in contemporary America, a comparison is instructive. In the ancient gymnasia, youths gathered to learn not only wrestling and running but philosophy and rhetoric. The gymnasia—where bodies were exercised, oiled, massaged, and bathed—created "a distinctive material setting for a highly textured, bodily pedagogy."[34] There students learned "a set of linked habits—the habits of discursive moves and wrestling moves, the habits of competing, pushing, developing, responding—linked if not in the mind, then certainly in the body."[35]

Although the modern court is not an explicit place of bodily training, law students learned how to embody client-empowering advocacy there. The situation in which Chloe found herself when her client fell to the floor, crying, required immediate bodily response. Although the client's action was understandable (especially when viewed through a feminist lens), it was dramatic and unusual—something that Chloe had not seen before. From a client-empowerment perspective, the situation required a physical recognition of solidarity (kneeling down beside her) and support (letting her cry). Chloe's act of speaking (telling the client that it wasn't her fault) was also an embodied act, not only because speaking is a physical phenomenon performed by one's mouth, lips, tongue, breath, and vocal chords, but because speaking can only be done from one's particular body, which is situated in a particular context (in this case, from an African American woman advocate in a suit kneeling down beside her client).

When faced with this situation, Chloe initially froze. She was prompted to embody the *mētis* required by client-empowering advocacy but hadn't yet developed the ability to respond intuitively on her own. As I discuss next, developing this kind of intelligence required performing similar but not identical acts repeatedly, under the guidance of a mentor.

Supervised Learning by Doing

In the court setting, in which no two advocacy situations are identical, an advocate must attend to appropriateness of time and place—what the ancient Greeks called *kairos*. While some rhetoricians have imagined *kairos* as the rational accommodation of the speaker to the objective circumstances of the speaking situation, others point to an "immanent, embodied, mobile, nonrational version," an understanding of which can be learned only through practice and performance.[36] For the ancient Greeks, an understanding of kairotic response developed through what Hawhee describes as "repeated encounters with difference—different opponents in different positions at different times and places."[37]

The court functioned in a similar way for law students. While abusive relationships can look similar to one another, no two clients are exactly the same or have the same goals or needs. And while judges follow more or less the same procedures in abuse prevention order hearings, no two judges do exactly the same things, and the same judge can act differently from day to day or hearing to hearing. The "repeated encounters with difference"—different clients, different judges, different circumstances—helped students understand clients as individuals and each rhetorical situation as unique. But the repetition of these encounters also helped students discern patterns that could inform their future kairotic responses. The repeated encounters helped advocates build up an encyclopedic memory on which to draw in any particular moment; an encyclopedic memory is key to "*mētis*'s ability to use . . . its treasure of past experiences and to inventory multiple possibilities."[38]

Some of these repeated encounters occurred with the student playing the role of observer—for example, sitting in court watching hearings while waiting for a client. Learning in this case happened through observation. As Samantha explained, "It helps that you work with more than one person while you're in court, because you see each other advocating and you pick up different things, like maybe I'll try that one when I'm advocating next time." In most of these encounters, however, the students learned by doing, performing advocacy with actual clients. They were prepared for these encounters in their preliminary training at the beginning of the semester through role-playing exercises that mimicked the pace and physical setting of hearings. In these exercises, students were assigned to play clients, defendants, or advocates and were provided accounts of the relationship from the perspective of the person they were playing or advocating for. (Each student had the opportunity to play the role of both advocate and client.) The instructor and supervising attorney played the role of judge and managed the pace of the hearing (as would an actual judge) through their questions. After each exercise, the instructor and students made suggestions for improving the performances. The hearings were held in the law school's mock courtroom so that students could physically occupy their roles. These role-playing exercises were essential to students' understanding of how to translate their theoretical knowledge of client empowerment into action.

Once at the court and working with actual clients, students required supervision. Chloe's supervisor, for example, played a key role in how she responded to her client who had fallen to the floor crying. Chloe's supervisor was physically beside her, whispering advice about what to feel ("Empathy, empathy, empathy"), what to do ("Get her, get her"), and what to say ("Tell her it's not her fault"). Without this guidance in the moment, Chloe would not have known how to perform the *mētis* required by client-empowering advocacy. No set of rules given beforehand could have substituted for this situated intervention. In this example, Chloe learned through direction. In other instances, students learned through imitation (by watching supervisors or fellow students in action) or correction (by being redirected from one path to another). But developing *mētis* means being able to work independently. Although Chloe could perform *mētis* in this particular moment with prompting, developing this intelligence as her own—so that it could emerge quickly and responsively—required repetition.

This repetition occurred over time in encounters with clients, judges, and others repeated over weeks so that it became a habit. As Hannah explained, "On Tuesday when I was in front of the judge, I felt like an actress. Who am I to argue in front of a judge? But it is also really cool. . . .I feel myself becoming an advocate." Initially, the role felt foreign, as if Hannah were unqualified to take it on. But the more she performed as an advocate, the more the role of advocate became part of her identity. James J. Murphy describes a similar goal in the rhetorical education of Aristotle and Quintilian, in which a "person *becomes* rhetorical" through habituation.[39] For Hannah, the identity was something that she experienced in an embodied way ("I *feel* myself becoming") and emerged over time (she was "*becoming* an advocate").

Students developed these habits through observation and simulation and then performance with actual clients in court. For the most part, these performances were practices that supported the rhetorical work of their clients. I describe these practices next.

Advocates Supporting the Rhetorical Work of Others

Students at the court engaged in activities that Kenneth Kolb, in his ethnography of advocates, describes as care work and legal work. Care work involved supporting clients personally and emotionally, including listening to them and helping them plan for their safety. Legal work involved explaining their legal options, such as participating in criminal prosecutions and seeking civil remedies such as abuse prevention orders.[40] In this section, I analyze all these activities as *support*; the advocates engaged in them in order to support the rhetorical work of their clients. By focusing on the clients' rhetorical work and the advocates' roles in supporting it, I hope to illustrate how the activities of both clients and advocates amount to coordinated and distributed advocacy that emerged as kairotic responses to particular situations.

Advocates typically met clients after they had come to court seeking an abuse prevention order. Anyone coming into a Massachusetts court seeking an order is directed to a clerk, who gives her a two-page complaint form to fill out (figures 2 and 3).[41] Often called a 209A after the state statute that gave rise to it, the complaint form was specifically developed "to permit a plaintiff to prepare and file such complaint *pro se*"—that is, on one's own behalf. In effect, the complaint transforms, simplifies, and reduces the language of the statute into a version intended to enable a layperson to apply for an order without an attorney. The advocates usually approached people as they filled out the forms, asking if they wanted help. The person would turn in the completed form to the clerk, who would compile it in a folder along with other documents (such as the defendant's criminal record and any hospital or police reports) to send to the judge sitting that day.

Advocates and clients usually waited in the courtroom or the hallway for their cases to be called. During the hearing itself, which usually lasted a few minutes, the client stood before the judge (usually with the advocate beside her), who would look over the complaint and other documents, ask questions, and render a judgment on the spot. Most initial hearings are *ex parte* (one party), meaning that the defendant is not present. If an order is granted, a copy

COMPLAINT FOR PROTECTION FROM ABUSE
(G.L. c. 209A) Page 1 of 2

COURT USE ONLY – DOCKET NO.

TRIAL COURT OF MASSACHUSETTS

A | ☐ BOSTON MUNICIPAL COURT ☐ DISTRICT COURT ☐ PROBATE & FAMILY COURT ☐ SUPERIOR COURT _____ DIVISION

B | Name of Plaintiff *(person seeking protection)*

F | Name of Defendant *(person accused of abuse)* | Defendant's Alias, if any

Sex: ☐ M ☐ F

C | ☐ I am 18 or older.
☐ I am under the age of 18, and
_____,
my_____ *(relationship to Plaintiff)* has filed this complaint for me.
☐ The Defendant is 18 or older.

G | The Defendant and Plaintiff:
☐ are currently married to each other
☐ were formerly married to each other
☐ are not married but we are related to each other by blood or marriage; specifically, the Defendant is my
_____
☐ are the parents of one or more children
☐ are not related but live in the same household
☐ were formerly members of the same household
☐ are or were in a dating or engagement relationship.

D | To my knowledge, the Defendant possesses the following guns, ammunition, firearms identification card, and/or license to carry:

E | Are there any prior or pending court actions in any state or country involving the Plaintiff and the Defendant for divorce, annulment, separate support, legal separation or abuse prevention? ☐ No ☐ Yes If Yes, give Court, type of case, date, and (if available) docket no.

H | Does the Plaintiff have any children under the age of 18?
☐ No ☐ Yes
If Yes, the Plaintiff shall complete the appropriate parts of Page 2.

I | On or about (dates) _____ I suffered abuse when the Defendant:
☐ attempted to cause me physical harm   ☐ placed me in fear of imminent serious physical harm
☐ caused me physical harm   ☐ caused me to engage in sexual relations by force, threat or duress

J | **THEREFORE, I ASK THE COURT:**
☐ 1. to order the Defendant to stop abusing me by harming, threatening or attempting to harm me physically, or placing me in fear of imminent serious physical harm, or by using force, threat or duress to make me engage in sexual relations.
☐ 2. to order the Defendant not to contact me, unless authorized to do so by the Court.
☐ 3a. to order the Defendant to leave and remain away from my residence: *See Plaintiff Confidential Information Form.*
If this is an apartment building or other multiple family dwelling, check here ☐
☐ 3b. to order the Defendant to leave and remain away from my workplace: *See Plaintiff Confidential Information Form.*
☐ 3c. to order the Defendant to leave and remain away from my school: *See Plaintiff Confidential Information Form.*
☐ 4a. to order that my residential address not appear on the order.
☐ 4b. to order that my workplace address not appear on the order.
☐ 4c. to order that my school address not appear on the order.
☐ 5. to order the Defendant to pay me $_____ in compensation for the following losses suffered as a direct result of the abuse:
_____
☐ 6. to order the Defendant, who has a legal obligation to do so, to pay temporary support to me. **(You may not obtain a temporary Order from a Boston Municipal, District or Superior Court if there is a prior or pending Order for support from the Probate and Family Court.)**
☐ 7. to order the relief requested on Page 2 of this Complaint pertaining to my minor child or children.
☐ 8. to order the following: _____
☐ 9. to order the relief I have requested, except for temporary support for me and/or my child(ren) and for compensation for losses suffered, without advance notice to the Defendant because there is a substantial likelihood of immediate danger of abuse. I understand that if the Court issues such a temporary Order, the Court will schedule a hearing within 10 court business days to determine whether such a temporary Order should be continued, and I must appear in Court on that day if I wish the Order to be continued.

DATE | PLAINTIFF'S SIGNATURE
X _____ | **Please complete affidavit on reverse of this page**

This is a request for a civil order to protect the Plaintiff from future abuse. The actions of the Defendant may also constitute a crime subject to criminal penalties. For information about filing a criminal complaint, you can talk with the District Attorney's Office for the location where the alleged abuse occurred.

FA-1 (1/12)   COURT COPY

2 | Massachusetts Complaint for Protection from Abuse (209A), page 1. *Source:* Commonwealth of Massachusetts, http://www.mass.gov.

is given to the client and to the police, who serve it to the defendant. To allow time for the defendant to be served with the order and to give the defendant an opportunity to confront the accuser, any orders granted at *ex parte* hearings in Massachusetts are good for only ten days. At that point, a two-party hearing determines if the order can be extended, usually for a year.

AFFIDAVIT	Describe in detail the most recent incidents of abuse. The Judge requires as much information as possible, such as what happened, each person's actions, the dates, locations, any injuries, and any medical or other services sought. Also describe any history of abuse, with as much of the above detail as possible.

On or about _____ , 20 ____ , the Defendant _____

_____

_____

_____

_____

_____

_____

_____

_____

_____

_____

_____

_____

_____

_____

_____

_____

_____

_____

_____

_____

_____

If more space is needed, attach additional pages and check this box: ☐

I declare under penalty of perjury that all statements of fact made above, including those provided on P.1, Section E and P.2, Sections A and B of the Complaint form regarding prior and pending court actions, and in any additional pages attached, are true to the best of my knowledge.

DATE SIGNED	PLAINTIFF'S SIGNATURE
	X _____

WITNESSED BY	PRINTED NAME OF WITNESS	TITLE OF WITNESS
X _____		

I have transcribed the above affidavit for the Plaintiff	☐ Court Certified Interpreter
_____ _____	☐ Court Screened Interpreter
Signature Print Name	☐ Other _____
	☐ Remote Translation Via Telephone/Video

3 | Massachusetts Complaint for Protection from Abuse (209A), page 2. *Source:* Commonwealth of Massachusetts, http://www.mass.gov.

Throughout this process, clients engage in a range of rhetorical practices. In what follows, I focus on how advocates supported clients in three broad categories of practice: (1) deliberating about what to do and how to do it, (2) establishing a presence in the courtroom, and (3) creating a credible *ethos*. As scholars in various fields have noted, the work of supporting others is often done by women and, as a result, often overlooked, devalued, or trivialized.[42] But supporting the rhetorical practices of others is a *techné*—an art—that requires more than meets the eye. In many cases, the support provided to clients also constituted rhetorical education for the clients themselves, as they learned more effective rhetorical practices.

Supporting the Client's Deliberation

Although the deliberative genre of rhetoric was first theorized by Aristotle as a *public* phenomenon marked by dialogue about best courses of action for the polis, individuals often engage in dialogue with themselves to decide what to do. Someone seeking an abuse prevention order must decide whether to file the complaint at all, how to define and represent her experience (for herself, for the defendant, and for a public audience), and how to continue to live her life (with or without the order) given the abusive situation that has brought her to court in the first place. The complaint form compels this deliberation but does not give much guidance about the implications of the various courses of action the plaintiff might choose.

To support the client's deliberation, the advocates in this program supplemented the form through listening metonymically. According to Ratcliffe, listening metonymically "helps listeners avoid the trap of unfair generalizations and stereotyping" because it "invites listeners to assume that one member of a group (say, one woman) does *not* speak for all other members (say, all women)."[43] A traditionally trained advocate might assume that anyone in an abusive relationship—and especially anyone who comes to court looking for an order—should file a complaint. But an advocate trained in client empowerment does not assume that all abusive relationships are the same or that abuse prevention orders are the solution for every situation. Chloe, for example, said that the court experience taught her that "domestic violence has no face . . . [because I've seen a] vast array of women . . . and how their stories were different." Chloe learned this perspective from repeated encounters with different clients.

At the same time, however, listening metonymically demands that the listener (here, the advocate) understand the client as a member of a class (here, those abused by intimate partners). The understanding that these individuals could constitute a class also emerged partially from the advocates' repeated encounters with different clients. Through repetition, the advocates began to see patterns across individual cases, and these patterns resonated with their classroom training, supervision, and reading. Advocates were thus able to bring a broader perspective when viewing the situations of individual clients who might have been isolated by their abusers and communities. Trained in client empowerment, these advocates felt compelled to help individual clients understand their situations from this broader perspective rather than simply echoing what the client already knew, believed, or wanted to hear. Here the advocates employed what Ratcliffe calls an "accountability logic," a move of rhetorical listening that "asks us to recognize our privileges and nonprivileges and then act accordingly."[44] For the advocates in this study, the primary privilege was knowledge of the legal system. With that privilege came the responsibility to both share knowledge with clients and ultimately defer to the clients' expertise. Chloe, for example, explicitly compared the idea of privilege in client-empowerment advocacy with traditional advocacy:

> Having this kind of knowledge and being able to give that information to someone else is really empowering too. The attitude of "I'm going to save the world" or "I'm going to save you"—that kind of mentality doesn't come across at the clinic. I feel very privileged and lucky to have this education and that I'm being taught so much that I can provide assistance to someone who's going through it, and in the end, they are going to make their own decision. . . . I feel privileged being able to go in front of judges, being able to learn a lot about the court system and expressing that to my clients.

For Chloe, the accountability demanded by the privilege of legal education meant sharing knowledge of the system with her clients so that they could use that knowledge for their own deliberations.

Hannah extended the idea of privilege to her knowledge about domestic violence and client-empowerment advocacy. She explicitly compared herself to the clerks who worked in the restraining order office, not just in terms of legal knowledge, but in terms of knowledge about domestic violence and client-empowering advocacy:

> We [advocates in the court clinic program] have the privilege of reading these wonderful manuals and having all these trainings and learning some of these dynamics of domestic violence, and restraining office clerks have

no training or very little training. They know nothing about safety planning and certainly nothing about client empowerment, because oftentimes if [the clerks are] not busy, they'll ask them a few questions and [the clerk will] check off no contact, no abuse, stay away from the kids, vacate the house, without (A) really explaining what the different kinds of relief are and (B) letting the client think about her safety and make active decisions about how she wants the restraining order to look. They just check, check, check, check, check. What happens oftentimes is that we'll get them after the clerk has already gotten to them and explain to them that you can ask for just a no-abuse order. [We tell them,] "You don't have to have him stay away from you if you want to keep talking to him," whatever it is, and they didn't even know that was an option because the clerk is just filling out forms.

The clerks described here exerted a power over the plaintiff that the advocates trained in client empowerment deliberately avoided or mediated. And, as in the hands of the advocate, the complaint form in the hands of the clerks was both agent and tool: it shaped human action and was used as a tool for human goals. Having no training in the client-empowerment philosophy, a clerk might have imagined that she was being helpful by filling out the form for a client. Doing so, however, markedly diminished the opportunities for the client to represent her own experience.

The client's opportunities to determine whether an order was the right decision were also diminished. Even though requesting the order was the reason she came to court, the client might have been ambivalent or might not have fully understood the implications of asking for or receiving an order. Advocates supported this kind of deliberation by what Grabill describes as helping people "make sense of their social (rhetorical) world."[45] Talia, for example, worked with a client who had been assaulted by her former boyfriend. The man had never been physically violent before the incident that brought the client to court. The client had filed a police report and had visible bruises and cuts on her hands from the assault. Talia remembered,

We got out the paperwork and she sees on the top "abuse prevention order" and she said, "I don't like that this says 'abuse.'" . . . I said, "There's other kinds of abuse than what you might be thinking of, like violent physical abuse." We talked about emotional abuse and verbal abuse and this controlling behavior and the fact that they're broken up and she should be able to see whoever she wants and he shouldn't be bothering her like this. That is a form of abuse. At that point she was like, "I don't know if this is what I want to do. He's not abusive." Then we were going back and forth. . . .She clearly still loved him. I believed her when she said he wasn't inherently violent and that he didn't have all these lethality factors that we think of in safety planning. . . .But at the same time, her idea of abuse was completely skewed. She didn't think that that situation was violence and yet she called the police. . . .Trying to explain to her . . . from the outside looking in, what would it look like. . . .She sat there and looked at it for a while. It was probably a few minutes. She checked it off herself, and I just didn't say anything else.

What the client checked off was in box I (see figure 2). From a legal perspective, this box provides the grounds for the order: the options listed—"attempted to cause me physical harm," "caused me physical harm," "placed me in fear of imminent serious physical harm," and "caused me to engage in sexual relations by force, threat or duress"—come directly from the definitions of abuse in chapter 209A of the Massachusetts General Laws. For this reason, a person must select one of these options to even be heard.[46] To respond at all to box I is to make an argument about definition: the client must first define her experience as abuse. Checking off a particular box requires making an argument about the nature of the abuse: Did the defendant actually cause physical harm or just threaten it? Was the client afraid? Was the abuse sexual? In some places, the client must engage in self-definition: at the very least, she "suffers"; if she selects the third checkbox, she is "in fear"; and if she selects the fourth box, she identifies as a victim of rape.[47]

The client's deliberation, then, was about whether her experience constituted abuse and, if so, what sort of abuse it was. In supporting this deliberation, Talia did not simply reflect back what the client had said. She instead offered other definitions of abuse and an alternative interpretation of the man's behavior based on a different perspective—someone looking at it from the outside. This perspective, like all perspectives, was an embodied way of seeing, as each person had different experiences. Talia's response emerged not from applying abstract rules learned elsewhere but from the immediate encounter between herself and the client while looking at the paperwork. Talia had read the client's body for signs of harm and therefore future risk (the bruises and cuts on her hands) and for signs of ambivalence (her hesitation at checking off the box).

Much of this work was about supporting the client's deliberation about her own safety. Hannah, for example, had a client who had come in for an order shortly after being attacked by her ex-boyfriend. The boyfriend had been arrested and arraigned that morning during a session that the client had observed. During the arraignment, the ex-boyfriend had made threatening gestures to the client from the custody box, and his new girlfriend had verbally threatened her from two seats behind. Hannah remembered that her client "was shaking. Her legs were shaking and her whole face was swollen as if she had been crying. . . . She was obviously very traumatized. When the [advocate from the DA's office] was talking to her, she was looking around, she was totally checked out. She wasn't listening at all. She was paranoid, but in a reasonable way, not [that] she was crazy paranoid. She was with reason very paranoid. She didn't know where the [defendant's] girlfriend was. She'd just been threatened [by the defendant's girlfriend, and] she had been attacked an hour or two before." Visual cues from the client's body gave Hannah an indication of her fear. Hannah's own experiences in the courthouse that day—she saw the defendant's girlfriend in the courtroom, and she saw the defendant in the custody box— helped confirm that her fear was real and immediate. Even if the defendant did not make bail, Hannah knew she needed to help the client plan how to remain safe from the girlfriend. Hannah got permission from the client to introduce her to the security guard so that she would feel safer inside the courthouse between hearings.

All the advocates said that helping clients plan for their own safety was the most important part of their job. During hearings, advocates routinely asked judges whether anything in a defendant's criminal record should make the client concerned for her safety. Advocates also helped clients with other needs (e.g., concerning housing, public benefits, or immigration) caused or exacerbated by the abuse. Their advocacy practices included writing letters (e.g., to the state public housing office explaining that the client was a victim of domestic violence and needed to be given priority on the waiting list), making phone calls (e.g., to shelters to locate available beds or employers to let them know why a client had missed work), and referring clients to other specialists. Samantha, for example, had a client who was six weeks pregnant and running from her ex-boyfriend. She had been on a public housing waiting list for five years and stayed for stretches with friends or family in the interim. In the incident that brought the client to court, the ex-boyfriend had stalked her as she was walking home and then assaulted her by punching her, choking her, and kicking her in the abdomen. Bystanders had witnessed the attack and called the police, but he had escaped arrest. With her supervisor, Samantha wrote a letter to the housing authority arguing that the client should be given priority because of the abuse. Samantha also followed up with the police to see whether the defendant had been served with the order and whether there was a warrant out for his arrest (because of the incident that brought the client to court).

Supporting a client's deliberation sometimes meant deferring to decisions that the advocate didn't agree with. In another case, Hannah's client had wanted to vacate an order, which Hannah thought was dangerous because the abuser had tended to obey orders when they were in place and become violent when they were not. The man had threatened to kill the client, threats that the client called empty. Hannah found it "really hard because she's in a dangerous situation, I'm concerned for her safety, and I also can't tell her what to do." She confessed, "Our egos want to be, 'I was the one who got her out of it,'" but she knew that telling the client what to do would just reinforce the client's sense of powerlessness. Hannah's strategy instead was to "ask her questions like, 'Why do you think that this time is going to be different than any of the other times?'" Hannah hoped that the client would rethink her situation, but she also wanted her to feel comfortable coming back to the courthouse, telling her, "There's absolutely no shame if you change your mind. Please come back. We will be here, and you will get the order again. Just because you changed your mind this time doesn't mean you can't come back and change your mind again."

In this regard, the client-empowerment model is very different from the dominant model of advocacy used not only by lawyers but by law enforcement officers. Chloe spoke specifically about these differences in reflecting on a client who was also working with a domestic violence detective. According to Chloe, the domestic violence detective was "telling [the client] what she should do . . . and ordering her to do this, that, and the other." The detective had said to the client, "You need to make sure that you get your locks changed, talk to this woman about getting it," and "after you stay with your mom, call the police station so they can escort you back to your house." The client-empowerment model, Chloe explained, meant helping a client see "what consequences or issues may arise and let[ing] her come to her own decision." Rather than telling the client to get her locks changed, Chloe asked her, "If he is vacated from the home, does he have keys? He may have the keys, and you may want to consider getting your locks changed." And rather than telling the client to stay with her mother, Chloe asked where she was staying that night, and she and the client discussed the alternatives.

Supporting the Client's Presence in the Courtroom

As I described earlier, students developed *mētis* through repeated interactions with others in the physical space of the court. Central to this embodied knowledge is understanding what to do with one's body in that space. Through repeated encounters, advocates learned how to read the semiotics of spaces and move meaningfully within them. Such "moving about" is "neither determined nor captured by the systems in which they develop," as de Certeau explains.[48] In other words, although advocates' movements "remain subordinated to the prescribed syntactical forms"[49] of the space—such as the locations where advocates may and may not go as well as when advocates are expected to occupy particular locations—advocates can make some choices about their movements (e.g., whether to kneel down with a client who is crying).

Like advocates, their clients must also move within the court, yet they are not (usually) practiced in doing so. While some clients may have previously been to court or sought abuse prevention orders, the process for some is a completely new experience. Unless they are advocates or attorneys themselves, even clients who have gone through the process before have not had the benefit of the repeated pedagogical activities (reading, reflection, and supervision) through which student advocates develop *mētis*. Before coming to a court for an order, many people would not even know that abuse prevention order hearings are public affairs, occurring in an open courtroom alongside arraignments, bail hearings, and the like, and that asking for an order involves standing before a judge in front of a gallery of spectators. The public nature of the hearing might not be clear even when someone is filling out the paperwork. Not knowing what happens physically—whether they will stand or sit, who else will be present, what they will be expected to say or do—can be a source of anxiety that occupies clients' attention. All the advocates noted that preparing clients to meaningfully occupy physical space during the hearing, including where to stand and what to do, was a central part of their role.

Preparing clients to occupy space in the courtroom was itself embodied action, often occurring in the courtroom. When possible, advocates sat with clients in the public gallery before their cases were called, using other cases to explain what their own hearings might look like. Samantha described her role as guide:

> I'll point those things out—"All right, this is a restraining order [hearing], that's what's going on right now"—just so they can see how it goes so that they know what to expect when they go up there in front of the judge....I [would tell clients], "The same thing that the judge is asking this person right now, they may ask you. Maybe [the judge will] vary it a little bit— depending on what they read in your affidavit, they may have other questions for you." Just so that [the client] can get a feel for it, and it's not this big tension of what's the judge going to say, what do I do, where do I put my hands—just [telling] them, "They are going to swear you in, the judge is probably going to read your information and not speak to you at first and then look up and say, 'Are you [so-and-so]?'" So they get a feel for what the process is going to be like versus me telling them what's going to happen. They at least get to see what it looks like.

Samantha's emphasis on helping clients "get a feel" for the hearing illustrates the intersection of physical embodiment and social action. As Pierre Bourdieu explains, getting "a feel for the game" is an embodied way of understanding how to navigate not only sports but all social situations.[50] For Samantha, "getting a feel" for the hearing was something that needed to happen *before* the hearing began as a method of preparation. Telling the client about the hearing was not enough; this preparation depended on her physical location in the courtroom, watching and listening to other plaintiffs interacting with the same judge that a client would appear before. These observations showed a client not only where to stand, how to stand, and when to move away but also how to identify routine actions of others (such as the judge not speaking to her at first) that did not have special meaning for her case. Without the anxiety of uncertainty (what Samantha calls a big tension) about her own actions and those of others, a client could more easily focus on answering the judge's questions.

Sitting with clients in the courtroom served other functions as well. The courtroom gallery is a public space, with all those with business before the court filling the benches. Those seeking abuse prevention orders might sit next to defendants awaiting their own hearings. Samantha imagined her clients thinking, "I'm a victim and I'm sitting next to a defendant. I don't really know how to feel about this." For a victim of abuse, sitting among defendants could imply that the system is treating her as guilty of something rather than as someone who needs the court's help. Samantha sat with clients to help them feel less like the system was against them. In one of Hannah's cases, sitting with a client served as a sign to others that the client was not alone. In this case (the one in which the defendant's new girlfriend was threatening the client from behind her in the audience), Hannah functioned as visual proof that the client had support. As Hannah remembered, the client "kept looking back [toward the girlfriend], and then she moved closer to me and put her arm behind me as if she wanted to show the perpetrator or the girlfriend or whoever that she had somebody with her, and we were whispering back and forth." This performance was a collaboration between the client and advocate, each playing her part. In this instance, the actions of client and advocate were both coordinated (i.e., done in relation to one another) and distributed (i.e., divided between them). The performance was aimed not at official court actors (such as the judge) but at an equally significant actor in the client's life.

Once a client's hearing began, the advocate and client embodied coordinated and distributed advocacy, with the advocate typically standing beside the client in front of the judge. They worked together but engaged in different actions, with the client typically answering questions from the judge and the advocate speaking strategically, if at all, and supporting the client through various physical movements, including simply being present. As Samantha said, "I think they feel better when we're up there. They don't feel like they're by themselves and everybody's staring at them while they are explaining this horrible situation and trying to be protected from that." Advocates sometimes touched their clients on the back during particularly difficult moments. Samantha watched a hearing in which the client was upset about testimony being provided by a witness. She remembered that "the advocate was rubbing her back, like, 'I need you to calm down, I know you're frustrated'—just trying to keep her calm, especially because . . . I knew she was stressed out, I knew she was upset." In another hearing, Talia touched a client on the back in support because she felt that her role did not allow her to do more. In that case, the defendant had brought an attorney, who was asking Talia's client upsetting questions. Talia recalled, "I couldn't really do anything because I'm not her attorney, I can't object. I stood there and tried to put my hand on her back and console her a little bit. I kept whispering, 'Just ignore him, don't even think about what he's asking.'" Advocates in Mary Schuster and Amy Propen's courtroom study provided the same kind of physical support while standing next to clients who were reading victim impact statements.[51]

When defendants were present at hearings, advocates stood between their clients and the defendants (who were often only several feet apart), serving as a physical and visual barrier. They learned this technique in the mock hearings conducted as part of their initial training. Through supervision, both Hannah and Chloe learned the limits of this kind of shielding. Hannah remembered wanting to walk one client to her car because she was afraid that the client's abuser might be waiting for her as she left the courthouse. She said, "That was a big no-no. . . . A couple times I got yelled at by [my supervisor] because I would want to walk them places. She was like, '(A) that's not your role, and (B) that's not safe.' I think a lot of that comes from my accompaniment background because that's exactly what our role was—to walk with people. But that's not what we're doing here." Similarly, Chloe remembered a client who started arguing with her abuser in a hallway in the courthouse. She recalled, "I tried to move her, put myself in front of her, and [my supervisor] said, 'Don't do that.'" Through performing (or attempting to perform) the act of shielding in these different instances, Hannah and Chloe were exposed to correction that helped them develop *mētis*. They learned not only how shielding could be appropriate but also when and where it might be.

For Hannah, helping clients establish a presence was about helping them gain access to power. She described her own access to this power in strikingly embodied terms, saying, "In the court, we're wearing a suit, we've got our official ID thing around our neck, we've got clipboards, [and] we're allowed by security in places that other people aren't." Calling it a privilege to have this kind of access, Hannah said that "everybody should know the things I get to learn in law school." She said,

> As advocates, the best that we can do is explain to people the process, who the different players are, how the legal system is set up to protect their rights, what the different risks are, [and] what the various options are. It's impossible to navigate this stuff. That's why law school is such a privilege. People are just expected to know how to access certain protections and certain rights, and it's this incredibly convoluted system and there's no handbook really, and in so much of it, you're not entitled to any kind of lawyer or advocate to help you navigate it. [In a] client-centered practice, I am not here to be your spokesperson. I'm here to be a megaphone.

Hannah's emphasis on "navigation" highlights the embodied ways that clients negotiate the legal system, that interacting with the system is not a purely intellectual exercise divorced from one's physical position in relation to others in particular spaces. For Hannah, recognizing her privilege meant being accountable for sharing her access, imagined in these complex ways, with others rather than using that access to speak for others. She imagined amplifying their speech (as a "megaphone") by sharing the knowledge of the system she had gained by virtue of her privilege. Part of this amplification involved helping the client establish a credible *ethos*, as I explain next.

Helping the Client Establish a Credible Ethos

As discussed in chapter 2, women face particular problems of credibility both in and out of legal settings. In the 1980s and early 1990s, task forces examining American courts found pervasive gender bias for both women attorneys and women appearing as parties before the courts, with women of color facing even greater discrimination than their white counterparts. The task forces found that women appearing as witnesses "face special hurdles: their credibility is readily questioned, and their claims of injury are undervalued."[52]

A number of women in Ptacek's study reported not being believed by the judge.[53] Hannah experienced such judicial incredulity firsthand. She remembered,

There was a horror story yesterday. . . .I could not believe this. My client had been punched in the face. She had been attacked: she'd been strangled, punched in the stomach, and burned with a curtain rod that he put on the stove on her arm. She was wearing a big jacket. I didn't see the burn, but I saw the scratches, and she had bruises and stuff on her arms. But she didn't have any bruises on her face, and in the affidavit, it said, "He punched me in my face." That was on Sunday and this is Tuesday, so it was two days later. The judge read the affidavit and said, "I see here that you are alleging that you were punched in the face, but I'm looking at your face right now, and you don't look like you've been punched in the face. I don't see any bruises or anything"—calling into question the fact that she [had] gotten punched because he couldn't see any bruises on her face. I was in shock. And the poor woman was like, "I don't bruise that easily. I went to the hospital, they told me I had some sort of internal bruise, but I guess I don't bruise that easily." This judge was denying orders left and right. He granted hers.

Although the judge's questions adhered to the judicial guidelines, which state that "it is essential that the court be satisfied that the evidence submitted is credible,"[54] he could have asked other questions that would not imply that the client was lying—for example, "Can you tell me about your injuries?"[55]

Because of these problems, one of an advocate's primary roles is to help the client establish a credible *ethos*, a role that Schuster and Propen address in their study of victim advocacy in domestic violence and child protection cases. Through courtroom observations as well as interviews with both advocates and judges, Schuster and Propen found that victims must past "certain truth tests" in order to be accorded credibility by the court. For those abused by intimate partners, the most significant of these tests was to leave the abuser; those who chose to stay were seen as less credible. One of the judges Schuster and Propen interviewed believed that all victims of intimate abuse were fundamentally damaged, saying that "only innately passive women were targeted by their abusers." Helping victims establish credibility before the court was one way that advocates helped "make sense out of chaos for these victims."[56]

The first opportunity that a client has for establishing a credible *ethos* with the judge is on the affidavit part of the complaint (see figure 3), which asks her to tell the story in her own words. The prompt asks for the "most recent incidents of abuse" as well as history of abuse and signals the kind of specificity required by beginning the story for her: "On or about _____, 20__, the Defendant _____ . . ." In her affidavit for an emergency restraining order, for example, Jennifer Martel wrote,

> Jared Remy and I got in an argument over visiting my friend who lives next door. I brought my daughter next door . . . with me. Jared continued to call my cell phone and yelled at me to come home. So I went back home alone without my daughter to talk. We continued to argue. Then Jared grabbed my neck and head and slammed my head into the bathroom mirror. Then I tried to get away so I pushed back and tried to leave. I went back next door and Jared followed me and banged on the door, then went back to our place to get the key and let himself in to my friend's house. I

asked him to leave but he continued to come in and yell at me so I feared for my safety and called the cops.[57]

Martel's affidavit clearly established the legal grounds for an order: Remy caused her physical harm and put her in fear of physical harm. The judge issued the emergency order.

Advocates learned through their training, observation, and encounters with judges that most turn to the affidavit almost immediately rather than studying the first page of the complaint form. Advocates thus saw the affidavit as crucial for presenting a convincing case; like the victim impact statements in Schuster and Propen's study, the affidavit (and the entire complaint) itself "has the potential to accomplish meaningful advocacy work."[58] One of Hannah's clients told her that she didn't want to write anything on the affidavit, saying that she just wanted the judge to look at the first page. Hannah "explained to her that the affidavit is really the only thing that the judge will look at. He gets the paper work, he turns it over, and that's what he looks at." She then offered to write down what the client said. Hannah remembered that the client "started talking a mile a minute, launching in. . . .It was extremely difficult for her to tell the story, but I had to keep stopping her and asking her to go back because I had to make sure it was her words. It was like I was rubbing salt in the wounds. I felt like I was sticking my finger in a wound asking her to please pause so that I could write it down."

Hannah supported her client not only by predicting what the judge might do (and saving the client unnecessary pain) but by taking dictation, using the actions of listening and writing to help the client craft a convincing *ethos*. Without an advocate, this client likely would have submitted the complaint without filling in the affidavit, in which case the judge would have asked her to tell the story during the hearing. As much pain as the client apparently experienced telling her story to Hannah, she probably would have experienced more pain telling it in open court. Her reticence seemed primarily about the act of writing, as she opened up immediately when telling her story verbally. Hannah's concern for the authenticity of the dictation ("I had to make sure it was her words") ultimately overrode her own squeamishness about causing more pain ("I felt like I was sticking my finger in a wound").

Helen saw the client telling the story in her own words as a key to what rhetoricians call *invention*, or discovering what to say. Helen noted that "when [clients] start writing, they write out things that they didn't necessarily tell me because they forgot or those aren't the words that they would use if I asked a question." For Helen, this process was vital to client empowerment because the client got to tell what *she* thought was important rather than what someone else did. Helen took an approach that balanced this freedom with guidance. She said,

> I don't look over their shoulder as they're writing it and go, "Maybe you should talk about this." But I say when they get started, "Here's the affidavit. The judge wants to hear about what's going on between you and the defendant. And they want to know specifically the most recent incident that happened and the most serious incident that happened. So you can write it on there and just talk about that." So if they came in because of the most recent incident, I'll say, "So you should say, on Saturday, this is what the defendant did." And then after they finish writing, I look it over, and if I think that there is more that could be put in there, I ask them about that. I'll go, "Do you feel comfortable talking about this?" And sometimes they don't. And sometimes they're like, "Yeah, oh yeah, I just forgot because I was writing all this other stuff." [Even] if there's a lot of gobbledygook the judge really doesn't want to know about, it's better to have that in there than to try to censor what the client wants to say.

Like Hannah, Helen predicted what the judge would want to hear and framed her advice in terms of this prediction, a tactic employed by the advocates in Schuster and Propen's study as well.[59] (All the advocates used this strategy. Talia explained why: "It's allowing them to write what they want to write but giving them a framework. I don't say, 'You should put'; I say, 'The judge likes.' For some reason, I feel like they are more likely to listen because what they care about in the end is getting the order.") But Helen seemed wary of a tendency of lawyers working in the traditional mode, as López puts it, to "tutor subordinated people on how to behave and think" to the extent that they learn to exclude "irrelevant" information.[60] For Helen, it was better for the client to have her say, even if the information was not something that the judge would want to hear.

Helping the client craft a credible *ethos* in the affidavit also helped the client prepare for the hearing. Chloe had a client whose roommate had threatened to shoot her. The affidavit was only three sentences: "I'm in fear, the defendant threatened to shoot me, and I'm in fear for my kid's safety." Chloe believed that the judge would find the story partially credible because of the part that said "the defendant threatened to shoot me." But because the affidavit was so short, Chloe thought the judge would have questions. She remembered, "So I prepared her for that. I [said], 'We need to go through what exactly happened because you are going to need to explain it to the judge—what [the defendant] said, what led up to it.'" Chloe's prediction was based not on abstract knowledge about what judges should do after reading an affidavit but on knowledge gained from physically being in the courtroom on many occasions, observing and interacting with different judges. Her prediction also led her to suggest a dress rehearsal before the hearing: an opportunity for the client to perform her speech before a sympathetic audience before going in front of a more skeptical one.

Advocates reported to me that they tried to remain silent during hearings, deferring to their clients. Silence, according to rhetorician Cheryl Glenn, "may well be the most undervalued and *under*-understood traditionally feminine site and concomitant rhetorical art," able to be deployed strategically for a range of purposes.[61] Often understood as the absence of speech, silence and speech are instead "inextricably linked and often interchangeably, simultaneously meaningful."[62] For the advocates in this study, silence helped enable the speech of their clients by deferring to their expertise. Remaining silent bolstered the credibility of clients by giving the impression that the client's story needed no supplementation or translation. As Helen put it, "With the judges that I've dealt with, they don't want to hear from me, and once I start talking, they just think I'm trying to get them away from asking questions of the client for whatever reason. Usually the client has enough to assert [her] own position." The work that advocates did to prepare clients for their hearings made asserting their own positions possible. As Talia explained, "Most of our work isn't during the hearing at all [but during] the preparation with them beforehand."

Some advocates also tutored their clients in the body rhetoric they would need to perform once standing before the judge. Samantha told one of her clients, "Don't roll your eyes. If you have the defendant contesting the restraining order, you may hear things that you don't agree with. Try not to let it affect your attitude. Try to keep a straight face but listen to them because the judge may ask you, 'Did you hear what the defendant said? How do you feel about that?' So try to listen actively without letting the expression take your face, because even though the judge is listening to the defendant, the judge is also looking at you." This strategy paid off. As Samantha related, "That seemed to go really well last Friday with one of my cases. . . . The judge was like, 'She's very composed, she's very calm, I think I'm going to extend her order.' . . . [He said to the defendant,]

'You're very aggressive, I need you to calm down, you're yelling right now, so it's obvious to me why she wants this order.'" This client evinced credibility through her body language. Problematically, however, she also had to evince victimhood, interpreted by this judge as a lack of aggression.

Another stereotypical feature of victimhood is fear, a thorny problem for advocates. According to the 209A statute, "fear of imminent serious physical harm" is one of the grounds for obtaining an order. However, the statute does not mandate that a person *must* satisfy this particular requirement; she could, for example, provide evidence for the defendant attempting to cause or causing physical harm. Nonetheless, judges often asked plaintiffs if they were afraid and denied orders if the answer was no. Knowing that judges sometimes required plaintiffs to admit feeling fear created an advocacy challenge. Helen explained why this judicial attitude was problematic:

> Some victims . . . come off as really strong. And they are really strong. So they say, "Yes, he beat me, but I pushed him back and I fought back." We were actually reading this article [in the course] about battered women and they're not battered women because they fight back. And [they'll say things like] "He knows not to come near me again because I'll kick the crap out of him" or "My boyfriend will be there and he'll get the shit beat out of him." In terms of validating and understanding, I totally understand that and she feels angry about what happened. Whether the judge wants to hear that or not is another thing. . . . The judges always think, If she's not in fear, then why is she here? If she doesn't put that, or even when the client testifies and then the judge specifically asks them, which has happened to other clients—they say, "Are you in fear for your safety?" and they say no. And you're like, uh-oh, now we've got to get involved. So it is this balancing act sometimes.

Schuster and Propen encountered a similar reaction from a judge in their study who described "'women who have had their noses broken and clumps of hair pulled out standing right in front of me . . . telling me they are not afraid.'"[63]

Helen said that the judges she observed focused on the criterion of fear more than any of the others, yet many clients were most resistant to checking off the box saying "placed me in fear of imminent serious physical harm." She remembered working with one client who had initially checked off "attempted to cause me physical harm" and "caused me physical harm" but not the box about fear.

When she asked about the "fear" box, the client said, "I don't really know if I want to check that one off." Helen said, "[I asked her,] 'Were you afraid of the physical harm that happened?' And she was like, 'Well, yeah.' . . . [I said,] 'I think the judge would want to see that, but it's up to you if you want to check it.' So she decided to check it, which sometimes I feel bad about and other times, I'm like, I know this is going to be an issue later if we go in front of the judge and she hasn't checked this off because he's going to ask her."

For clients, the encounter with a judge could be new and intimidating. Even those who had gotten previous abuse prevention orders could find the experience uncomfortable or frightening. They might have forgotten the strategies they discussed with the advocate only a few minutes before. One strategy of support from the advocate, then, was nudging (e.g., whispering to a client to remind her of something that they discussed before the hearing). When a judge was talking about whether the client wanted the defendant to have contact with her children, Talia, for example, "pointed to my notes about the friend [who could help with visitation], so she brought it up." Another strategy was to pull the client aside, as Helen did with a client who was not telling the judge about the physical abuse she had endured. As Helen remembered, "I actually had to take a moment to say, 'Your Honor, can I talk to my client for a second?' And I reiterated that the judge want[ed] to hear about the physical things" even if they were difficult for the client to say. Both these strategies—nudging and pulling aside—were intended to guide the client without taking over for her.

In some contexts and in some moments, however, advocates did directly intervene. The written materials provided in training advise taking "a far more active role in hearings than contemplated by" the judicial guidelines. The writers continue, "We are not confident that judges are sufficiently trained in the dynamics of abuse, the 209A statute, or the interpretations and procedures set forth in the [judicial guidelines] to justify a practice where advocates remain silent supporters of their clients."[64] Besides suggesting both whispering in the ears of clients and pulling them aside, these materials urge advocates "in the most difficult of situations" and "only if she clearly needs and consents to this oral support" to present facts for the client. The materials also urge advocates to help clarify legal issues if necessary.[65]

According to one of the supervising attorneys, intervening when appropriate was challenging for students because it meant learning that deferring to clients doesn't mean being passive. Ways of intervening were practiced in early simulations. For example, students practiced asking in simulated hearings whether the defendant's criminal record (which the judge could see but the plaintiff and advocate could not) contained anything worrying for the plaintiff (such as a history of violence or ignoring restraining orders). Plaintiffs themselves would not know to ask this information; advocates could bring this expertise to bear, thus helping the plaintiff (and others) make informed decisions. Early in the clinic program, Chloe drew on the simulation experience by accompanying a client to the bench, where a judge had summoned her in order to protect her privacy. After the judge questioned the client about her affidavit, Chloe "jumped in and asked" about the defendant's criminal record (which apparently did not indicate a history of violence). She then followed up to make sure that the defendant would vacate and give up keys to the apartment, as well as surrender any weapons, all of which the judge confirmed.

Learning when to intervene was a matter of supervision and practice. In one case, Helen had a client who wanted to extend an existing order for another year. The defendant was contesting the extension, and during the hearing, the judge asked the client if the defendant had contacted her during the past year. When the client said no, the judge (in an unusual move) said that he wanted to think about it and scheduled a second hearing for later in the day. To Helen, the fact that the defendant had not contacted the client meant that the order was working. Helen was concerned that the judge thought that the order was no longer necessary. Between the two hearings, then, Helen consulted with her supervisor; together, they looked up the language of the statute and the judicial guidelines, which Helen took with her into the second hearing. She remembered,

> The judge asked the client, "Is there anything else you want to say?" She's like, "Yes, we had a long previous history of abuse. I don't want any contact with this man. He's been staying away." And then the judge looked at me, like what was I doing there with this paperwork, and I said, "Your Honor, under the statute, the fact that the defendant hasn't contacted her in the past year shouldn't inhibit her from asking for another one-year order. I have the statute and judicial guidelines here if you'd like to look at them." Which was a little ballsy, but I was a little pissed. He was like, "I know what the law is." But he granted her the extension. It was a six-month extension, which was stupid, but she got the extension. So that was an example of where the judge was already annoyed with us for being there and then he was even more annoyed that I did that. We had to do that for the client. We had to do that to put on the record that he was wrong.

In this situation, the judge seemed convinced by the truth value of the client's statement but uncertain of its significance. Helen, the advocate, filtered the client's statement through the statutory language and judicial guidelines, showing not only its credibility but its relevance. By Helen's account, her act of holding paperwork served as a flag to the judge that he should ask for her input. Once she indicated what the paperwork was—the guidelines that the judge was supposed to follow in these proceedings—the judge acquiesced.

Advocates also intervened when clients were not able to present a case that the judge understood. One of Talia's clients embodied a distinctly different *ethos* in the hearing than she had alone with her. The client, she said, "was very smart when I was talking to her. She was a history major, she's graduated from college, she's going into the Peace Corps, she's got a lot going for her. In interviews with her, you could tell that she had a very wide vocabulary, was very proficient." But in the hearing, the woman "was very timid and shy," so she didn't do a very good job answering the judge's questions. At this point, Talia stepped in to clarify, drawing from her interview with the client to help her make her case. In this instance, Talia served almost as a ventriloquist, repeating what the client had told her in private but was unable to say in public.

In a different case, Samantha intervened for a client not because the client wasn't presenting her case well but because the client and judge were talking past each other. She had a client in her twenties who had gotten a ten-day restraining order against her father. At the end of the ten days, she appeared again to extend the order for a year. Although temporary orders can be granted without the defendant there, longer orders require that the defendant be present or at minimum be served notice of the hearing. The client's father was not present at the second hearing, so the judge announced that he would not extend the order for a year because the police were never able to serve him notice. As Samantha explained to me,

[The judge] was like, "We haven't been able to serve him. . . .Is this the right address?" She's like, "Yes, he's home with my mother." He's like, "Well, now I'm confused." I'm like, "No, wait, it may say there's no service, but her mother called her and told her [that her] father was not coming to court. Her mother also had a restraining order and dropped her order against her father and told her [that her] father didn't think it was necessary for him to come to court. So he has notice. Even though it says that there was no service, he has notice. He knows about the court date. He's just been evading the service when they come to the house." After that, [the judge] started reading her affidavit a little more closely and was like, "This is your real father?" She said yes. He said, "And he tried to take the caps off your tires?" She said, "Yes, he tried to deflate my tires so I couldn't leave." He asked, "You fled the house?" And she said, "Yes, I fled the house, and they don't know where I'm staying right now." He said, "Okay, we're going to extend your order for a year."

In this moment, Samantha selectively performed a central rhetorical act of the traditional lawyer, what James Boyd White identifies as the translation of ordinary experience into the technical language of the law.[66] The client did not know that the most important information she had (for legal purposes) was that her father knew about the hearing. The word *serve* did not signal to the client that she needed to explain that her father knew about the hearing. The judge did not understand why the father had not been served if he lived at the address the police were given. Samantha was able to bridge this gap in understanding by translating between them. Yet her translation did not replace the voice of the client; it supplemented it. Advocacy was coordinated and distributed among the client, the advocate, and the complaint.

In the court context, advocacy was not limited to those actions performed by the person called advocate but was distributed among various actors. Some of these advocacy practices are more obvious than others and align more closely with traditional understandings of advocacy. A client speaking on her own behalf in front of a judge, for example, performs advocacy as traditionally conceived. However, judicial demeanor can serve to bolster or diminish the claims of clients or defendants, even though judges are often thought of as arbiters rather than advocates, as Ptacek has shown. Court staff—clerks, bailiffs, and so on—and police officers similarly can perform as advocates (rather than adversaries) by facilitating (rather than denying) services and believing (rather than denying) claims. The complaint form also performs advocacy functions, both through its very existence (as an enactment of legislation designed to give abuse victims a way of accessing judicial protection without an attorney) and through its representation of the client's story to the judge. And an abuse prevention order, if granted, serves an advocacy function by circumscribing abusers' actions through judicial words, backed up by institutional force.

This chapter has shown that advocacy actions are not only distributed across various actors but, in many instances, coordinated among them. I have focused here on the interaction of clients and advocates to illustrate that effective coordination is not given but arises from practice, supervision, reflection, and repetition. Advocates learned to embody the role of advocate by *performing* as advocates, in concert with a range of clients and before a range of judges. Over time, these performances, bolstered by theoretical understandings and corrected through supervision, helped students develop the attention to *kairos* necessary for embodied intelligence.

Conclusion | Lessons

In this book, I have described programs at the Domestic Violence Institute (DVI) at Northeastern University School of Law as an exemplar of rhetorical education in embodied advocacies. I suspect that most clinical legal education (CLE) programs embrace at least some of the goals and methods of the pedagogy described here. Because they usually serve real clients with real legal problems, clinics help students develop a facility in a range of advocacy practices. Often serving a disadvantaged clientele, clinical programs across the country are increasingly interested in helping students learn to communicate across difference, embracing listening and nonverbal communication as important practices.[1] Other features of the DVI programs may be unique, such as preventing students from engaging in traditional acts of advocacy, which helped students at both the hospital and the courthouse learn to listen rhetorically and see clients as experts in their own lives. Future research might investigate how other clinical programs invite students to embody the role of advocate.

Evaluating the DVI programs as rhetorical education invites a comparison to the rhetorical education provided by traditional law school curricula. While the DVI programs focused on producing rhetors, employed a range of embodied pedagogies, and emphasized communicating across difference, the rhetorical education provided by traditional law school curricula instead focuses primarily on producing legal knowledge, emphasizes form and authority rather than morality and social context, and positions legal language as a neutral arbiter of conflict.[2] In other words, the rhetorical education provided by law schools, on the whole, ironically seeks to distance itself from rhetoric.

An anecdote told by law professor Patricia J. Williams testifies to the dominance of that approach and her efforts to combat it in one of her courses:

> Walking down Fifth Avenue in New York not long ago, I came up behind a couple and their young son. The child, about four or five years old, had

evidently been complaining about big dogs. The mother was saying, "But why are you afraid of big dogs?" "Because they're big," he responded with eminent good sense. "But what's the difference between a big dog and a little dog?" the father persisted. "They're *big*," said the child. "But there's really no difference," said the mother, pointing to a large slathering wolf-hound with narrow eyes and the calculated amble of a gangster, and then to a beribboned Pekinese the size of a roller skate, who was flouncing along just ahead of us all, in that little fox-trotty step that keep Pekinese from ever being taken seriously. "See?" said the father. "If you look really closely you'll see that there's no difference at all. They're all just dogs."³

Williams surmises that the parents must be lawyers, asking, "How else do people learn to capitulate so uncritically to a norm that refuses to allow for difference?" To their child, big dogs *were* different from little dogs. But his point of view was irrelevant to the category of "dog" that seemed self-evident to his parents. Williams told the story to students in a seminar on women and property "to illustrate the rhetoric of power relations" in representations of reality, both in everyday life and in legal discourse and pedagogy. Through such rhetoric, she says, people are "taught not to see what they see."⁴

The DVI programs taught students that point of view matters in relation to advocacy because of the experiences of both clients and advocates. Based on my analysis of their programs, I propose the following theory of embodied advocacies:

+ *Advocacies are plural and distributed across actors.* In any given advocacy situation, multiple people can engage in various practices that interact with one another; thus advocacy can be understood as distributed across people and texts. In this study, advocacy practices were performed by students, lawyers, clerks, judges, doctors, nurses, and documents, as well as by clients and their friends and family.
+ *Advocacies are composed of a range of embodied rhetorical practices.* These practices include not just speaking and writing but also listening and using silence and physical movement, as well as supporting the rhetorical practices of others. In the client empowerment approach described in this book, listening is central because it validates another person's perspective.
+ *Advocacies are partial.* Every advocate, and every person being advocated for, has a point of view; there is no neutral place from which to advocate or to

determine the correct course of action. Because advocacy practices are informed by personal, disciplinary, professional, social, and cultural perspectives, they are necessarily incomplete. In domestic violence advocacy, clients bring their unique perspectives on their abusers, while advocates bring knowledge of patterns of abusive actions and their risks.

+ *Advocacies have material consequences that differentially affect advocates and those being advocated for.* In domestic violence advocacy, the most obvious consequences concern the physical safety of the client or the client's children. But advocacies can affect clients in other material ways as well, including housing, financial support, and access to medical care.

+ *Advocacies are relational and fluid.* Their dynamics depend on the embodied subjectivities of the people involved as well as dynamic contexts. Domestic violence advocates work across a range of identity categories and on problems that do not look the same from day to day. Rapidly changing conditions in housing, employment, and abuser behavior can affect a victim's choices and prospects.

+ *Advocacies are political.* Embodied subjectivities are both unique (in that no one has had the exact same experiences as anyone else) and part of multiple collectivities that are imbricated in relations of power. In domestic violence work, an advocate aware of assumptions about victims (e.g., that they don't fight back) might directly challenge these assumptions, potentially changing how others (such as a judges) view victims in the future.

+ *Advocacies occur in fluid temporal and spatial contexts in which advocates engage in embodied interactions with others.* Spaces shape and respond to the actors and activities within them. In this study, courthouses and hospitals presented both opportunities and constraints for advocacy practices.

These insights have implications for rhetorical education in advocacy, especially in law schools. In legal education, a pedagogy based on the theory I have advanced here challenges the traditional model of legal advocacy, in which an attorney (by virtue of legal knowledge and expertise) is the primary actor, advancing written and spoken arguments in legal forums. As the DVI programs illustrate, students may resist challenges to the traditional model. Through cultural representations of lawyers and legal practice, the law students at the DVI were already enculturated into a traditional model of advocacy. Explicitly comparing different models of advocacy (with discussions about their assumptions and possible outcomes) might help make students aware that the traditional model is not the only one available.

A pedagogy based on this theory of embodied advocacies should help advocates understand that their own perspectives are incomplete and that clients have expertise in their own lives. This book has offered rhetorical listening as a central strategy for achieving this pedagogical goal. In the DVI programs, students learned three moves associated with rhetorical listening: (1) creating identifications not just across commonalities but also across differences, (2) analyzing the cultural logics that inform claims as well as the claims themselves, and (3) employing a logic of accountability. Because the DVI's pedagogy did not draw on rhetorical theory, these moves were not named or isolated for practice. Clinical educators could explicitly use Ratcliffe's work to help students learn these moves.[5] Clinical educators could also draw on the work of other rhetoricians writing about rhetorical listening or methods for examining arguments and their foundational assumptions.[6] Explicitly naming and having students deliberately practice such skills can help motivate students and organize their learning.[7]

Explicitly teaching rhetorical listening and the evaluation of arguments can help decenter speaking as the standard activity of advocacy. While speaking for others is sometimes necessary, a pedagogy of embodied advocacies helps students recognize a wide range of practices. In legal education, advocacy is customarily defined as speaking on behalf of clients before decision-making bodies, such as courts. The prestige of participating in moot courts (in which students prepare for and participate in simulated court proceedings) speaks to the power of dominant images of lawyers as courtroom warriors.[8] A pedagogy of embodied advocacies would recognize not just speaking and writing but also other rhetorical actions, such as listening and using silence and physical movement in addition to supporting the rhetorical practices of others. Learning to use silence seems particularly helpful for lawyers, not just because it can facilitate rhetorical listening, but also because it can function as argument and exert power.[9]

Ideally, students would recognize this wide range of rhetorical actions and practice them in settings that allow them to develop embodied intelligence, or *mētis*. By virtue of their purpose of serving real clients with real legal problems, CLE programs are exemplars in this regard. As the DVI programs illustrate, practical settings offer students the "repeated encounters with difference" that help them learn to respond flexibly to the demands of particular moments.[10] Faculty developing practical experiences need to consider how particular settings further the pedagogical aims of their program. The DVI's hospital program, for example, provided an ideal setting for disorienting students and preventing them from engaging in advocacy practices. This setting also offered a rich environment for explicitly juxtaposing traditional conceptions of advocacy with their alternatives.

While I have formulated these propositions in the context of legal education, they might extend to other fields, as rhetorical education in advocacy occurs wherever someone learns rhetorical practices that perform support for another, even if these practices are not specifically identified as rhetoric.[11] Future investigations might explore how client empowerment, the advocacy approach embraced by the DVI, is understood and taught in other fields, such as social work and medicine, both of which have a well-established interest in this approach as well as listening as a key strategy.[12] Because of differing histories, disciplinary assumptions, and professional demands, the shape of rhetorical education in advocacy will be different in each field and each educational site.

For the present, this book has sought to inspire more conversations between rhetoricians and those who teach in law schools.[13] By both reconnecting with our shared history and forging new connections with contemporary rhetorical theory and practice, legal educators may be able to address concerns that law schools are not adequately preparing future attorneys to reach out into the world. Rhetorical theories and pedagogical approaches—which emphasize audience, context, and the social construction of reality—can help law students connect legal texts to human dilemmas in all their complexity.[14]

In turn, rhetoricians have much to learn from legal education. While rhetoric's ancient connection to law is part of every rhetorician's training, we have ignored much of what has followed. We should study the shift in nineteenth-century American law schools away from rhetoric and toward a "scientific" approach to legal education, a shift that probably contributed to the current disciplinary divide between the two fields. We need to pay attention to the modern law school as well. With the exception of legal writing curricula, rhetoricians have mostly ignored the rhetorical education of lawyers.[15] We need to learn more about the case method, investigating how its dominance in legal curricula affects how students understand the relationship of rhetoric to law, including their role as rhetors. We need to investigate how extracurricular activities such as editorial work on law reviews or moot court competitions shape how students understand the production of legal knowledge and the nature of advocacy. We need to explore experiential learning in law schools not just in

legal clinics but in simulations, labs, clerkships, externships, and residencies—
the ecologies where students learn to perform as rhetors.

And educators in rhetoric and law have a broad shared interest—namely,
producing citizens with the capacity for engaging responsively and responsibly
with others. Legal educators produce professionals who serve not just their clients but also, as officers of the legal system, the greater public good.[16] As Gerard
Hauser reminds rhetoricians, the role of producing responsible citizens has
been rhetoric's birthright since antiquity.[17] This birthright also belongs to law.
We should reclaim it together.

Appendix A | Research Methods

Although my formal study of the Domestic Violence Institute (DVI) did not begin until 2009, I attended their annual one-day conference on domestic violence in both 2007 and 2008 because of my long-standing interest in legal responses to women's issues. After the 2008 conference, I started to see possibilities for a research project with the hospital program, which emerged over the next few months in consultation with then director Lois Kanter. During my research with the hospital program (September 2009–April 2010), my plans for a study with the court clinic took shape. I conducted research with that program from December 2010 through February 2011.

I used ethnographic methods, primarily interviews and observations, to study both programs.[1] I recruited students through email sent to all program participants. For the hospital program, I interviewed two sets of students: those who interviewed women at the hospital (called "interviewer advocates," or IAs) and those who served as team leaders. I interviewed nine IAs three times (once before the program began, once after their first shift at the hospital, and once toward the end of the program). I interviewed a tenth IA twice; she dropped out of the program after the second interview and declined to be interviewed a third time. Five team leaders also took part; I interviewed them once. For the court program, I interviewed five students twice, once after their first shift at the court and once toward the end of the program.

Interviews with both sets of students followed a semistructured, qualitative format. My goal was to allow the respondent to direct the course of the interview as long as the material seemed potentially useful to the study. I followed the advice of Robert S. Weiss in *Learning from Strangers* by preparing a rudimentary guide of topics to be covered (reproduced at the end of this appendix) and using a range of techniques to help respondents develop information. Interviews lasted from forty-five minutes to an hour and a half.

I transcribed about half of the forty-four interviews. The rest were transcribed by a dedicated team of undergraduate research assistants and work-study students. To analyze the transcripts, I adapted a two-part coding method described by Robert M. Emerson, Rachel I. Fretz, and Linda L. Shaw in *Writing Ethnographic Fieldnotes*. In the first part (what they call open coding), I annotated the transcripts line by line with descriptive notes. Open coding allowed me to construct patterns and themes in the interview data. In the second part (what they call closed coding), I went back through the transcripts to assign codes developed from these patterns and themes. I did open coding in Microsoft Word and closed coding using Dedoose, a web-based application for analyzing qualitative and mixed-methods data. For some of the coding, I was assisted by an undergraduate researcher.

I conducted observations for a total of about 130 hours across both programs. I spent more than a third of that time shadowing a team of six (plus a team leader) at Boston Medical Center. The team worked one six-hour shift approximately every other week from October 2009 to April 2010 for a total of ten shifts; I observed nine of the ten shifts. I also conducted observations at the annual conference, meetings of team leaders in the hospital program, and an intensive week of training for students in the court program. I conducted several observations at the courts where the students worked. To help protect the attorney-client privilege that applied to the students' work, I did not observe hearings in which they participated.

In addition to interview and observation data, I collected and read narratives written by all ten students in the hospital program after their interviews. I also collected and analyzed pedagogical materials, including manuals covering domestic violence, client-empowering advocacy, and processes at the hospital and the court.

First Interviews with IAs

1. Reasons for applying to program
   a. How did you come to apply to the program?
   b. Develop experiences, thoughts, and feelings regarding victims, perpetrators, domestic violence, and responses to domestic violence from legal system, criminal justice system, and communities.

2. Expectations for work in program
   a. What do you expect to do?
   b. Develop thoughts and feelings about their roles/identities in relation to clients and legal/other systems.

c. What do you hope to gain from this experience?

d. Develop thoughts/feelings about advocacy and identity.

Second Interviews with IAs

1. First day at Boston Medical Center
   a. Walk me through your first shift.
   b. Describe how you approached your interviews.
   c. What was it like to listen? Did you hear anything that surprised you?
   d. Were you able to identify with any of the women? Along what lines?
   e. What were the barriers to talking to the women?
   f. What was it like to write the narrative?

2. Roles and expectations
   a. How do you see your role at Boston Medical Center? Is that different from before you started?
   b. What are your expectations/goals for the next shift?

3. Training
   a. What did you think of *Defending Our Lives*?
   b. What did you learn about domestic violence during the conference/training?
   c. Can you think of anything else related to your experience so far that I haven't asked you about?

Third Interviews with IAs

1. Concrete experiences
   a. Walk me through your last shift.
   b. Tell me about your best/worst experience.
   c. Tell me about any service that you took part in.
   d. Develop thoughts and feelings regarding listening, advocacy, domestic violence, victims, writing narratives, modeling/mentoring, and client-empowerment model.

2. Connections between program and rest of law school experience
   a. To what extent does what you're learning in this program connect with the rest of law school?

b. Develop thoughts and feelings regarding purposes of legal education and experiential learning.

3. Reflections
   a. Did the experience meet your expectations?
   b. How do you now see your role in the program? Is that different from when you started?
   c. Has your understanding of domestic violence / community responses / police and legal responses changed?
   d. Has your understanding of advocacy or lawyering changed?
   e. Have your long-term career goals changed?
   f. Can you think of anything else related to your experience that I haven't asked you about?

Interviews with Team Leaders

1. Reasons for becoming a team leader
   a. How did you come to be a team leader in the program?
   b. Develop experiences, thoughts, and feelings regarding victims, perpetrators, domestic violence, responses to domestic violence from legal system, criminal justice system, and communities.
   c. Develop thoughts and feelings about the legal system and their own role.

2. Latest day at Boston Medical Center
   a. Walk me through your last shift / most challenging shift.
   b. Develop thoughts and feelings regarding service cases.
   c. Develop thoughts and feelings regarding how group has changed over time, group interactions, and how IAs are learning.

3. Supervisory work
   a. Describe IAs' skills in listening and interviewing.
   b. What role do the written narratives play in the IAs' experiences?
   c. Reflection on work in program
   d. What have you gotten out of this experience?
   e. Develop thoughts and feelings regarding domestic violence, advocacy, and so on.

First Interviews with Court Advocates

1. Goals for the Domestic Violence Court Clinic course
   a. How did you come to enroll in the course? Goals?
   b. Develop motivations as they relate to advocacy, understandings of the legal / criminal justice systems, and domestic violence.
   c. Develop motivations as they relate to long-term career goals.

2. First day at court
   a. Tell me about your first day at the court.
   b. Develop thoughts and feelings regarding listening, advocacy, understandings of the legal / criminal justice systems, and domestic violence.
   c. Develop thoughts and feelings regarding legal solutions to domestic violence versus nonlegal solutions.
   d. Tell me about the process of filling out restraining order (209A) applications (refer to blank 209A form).
   e. Develop thoughts and feelings regarding translating victims' experiences into legal categories and language.

3. Training
   a. Did you feel prepared for this experience?
   b. Do you think differently about the program, your role, and domestic violence after training?

4. Expectations
   a. What are your goals for the next shift and the term?
   b. Develop thoughts and feelings regarding advocacy role.

Second Interviews with Court Advocates

1. Advocating for clients
   a. Walk me through process of advocating for a memorable client / a client whose application seemed straightforward / a client whose application seemed difficult.
   b. Develop thoughts and feelings regarding listening, advocacy, understandings of the legal / criminal justice systems, and domestic violence.
   c. Develop thoughts and feelings regarding legal solutions to domestic violence versus nonlegal solutions.

    d. Develop thoughts and feelings regarding translating victims' experiences into legal categories and language.

2. Restraining order process
   a. Tell me about the process of filling out restraining order (209A) applications (refer to blank 209A form).
   b. Develop thoughts and feelings regarding translating victims' experiences into legal categories and language.

3. Connections between Boston Medical Center program and court clinic
   a. For students who took part in the Boston Medical Center program, ask about connections between that program and the work they did in the court clinic.
   b. Develop thoughts and feelings regarding the connection between listening and advocacy.

4. Goals
   a. What are your current career goals? How does this program fit in with them?
   b. Develop thoughts and feelings regarding advocacy.

Appendix B | Interview Participants

This appendix gives biographical information for the students who participated as interviewers in the hospital program, along with those who served as advocates in the court program. All names are pseudonyms.

The following students interviewed women at the hospital:

+ Jonathan, twenty-nine, was a first-year law student who identified as white and Catholic. He had worked as a journalist for nine years before law school and was interested in civil rights law. When I asked him why he applied to the hospital program, he said that journalists "spend a lot of time observing and writing" but not making things better. The hospital program was an opportunity for him to "do something rather than just be more of an independent observer." As a journalist, Jonathan had covered several stories involving domestic violence. Growing up in a rural, low-income community, he was aware of abusive relationships among his high school classmates and their families.

+ Jessica, twenty-three, was a first-year law student who identified as Mexican American and "moderately Christian." She came to law school with the goal of working in either juvenile justice or family law. Jessica became interested in the hospital program after doing social work for two years in an Eastern European country with no legal or social services for those abused by intimate partners. She had no personal experience with domestic violence but had a close friend involved in a controlling and verbally abusive relationship.

+ Hannah, twenty-six, was a first-year law student who identified as white and Jewish. After graduating from college, she had worked as a human rights accompanier in Central America. She had also done intake for a legal aid office. She was motivated to attend law school and become involved with the Domestic Violence Institute (DVI) because of a desire to help victims of violence and others gain access to the justice system. Hannah had met women abused by intimate partners in her work as a human rights accompanier but had no other direct experiences with domestic violence. In her second year of law school, she participated in the court clinic program and my study of that program.

+ Liz, twenty-four, was a third-year law student who identified as white and nonreligious. She attended law school because of a desire to do public service work, and she enrolled in the hospital program because of a long-standing interest in domestic violence and women's issues. As an undergraduate at a women's college, Liz had worked as a resident assistant, counseling women on relationships and sexual health. She had been in a controlling relationship herself, had friends in verbally abusive relationships, and had an aunt in a marriage that involved gun violence.

+ Kim, twenty-five, was a first-year law student who identified as a white, nonpracticing Catholic of Irish descent. The desire to combat domestic violence was her primary motivation for attending law school and participating in the hospital program. As an undergraduate, she had worked as a victim witness advocate in a district attorney's office. Her father had beaten her mother, destroyed sentimental belongings, and threatened suicide. Her mother left when Kim was two years old. Kim's father went on to physically abuse a subsequent girlfriend; he died during an act of retribution aimed at the girlfriend for having him arrested for abuse. While Kim shared with me the details of this act, I have refrained from describing them in order to protect her identity.

+ Kelly, twenty-four, was a first-year law student who identified as white and culturally Jewish. She applied to the hospital program because of an interest in women's health care. Kelly attributed her interest in public service to her parents' occupations, her father being a police officer and her mother a public school teacher. Prior to law school, she had worked as a staffer for a member of the US Congress. She left because she wanted to "be on the ground helping people" rather than being part of a "faceless bureaucracy." She had no direct or secondhand experience with domestic violence.

+ Roberto, twenty-two, was a first-year law student who identified as Mexican American and Catholic. He was motivated to attend law school and participate in the hospital program because of a desire to help children and victims of sexual violence. His mother had been molested by a relative and physically abused by Roberto's father (before Roberto was born), and a number of his friends had been sexually assaulted.

+ Gretchen, twenty-five, was a second-year law student who identified as white and nonreligious. She had a long-standing interest in women's reproductive rights and had done grassroots work for several activist organizations. Before attending law school, Gretchen had worked as a paralegal. Calling herself "more punitive than most," she hoped to become a prosecutor after graduation to punish perpetrators of violence. She had no direct or secondhand experience with domestic violence.

+ Alexandra, twenty-five, was a first-year law student who identified as white and Catholic. She was motivated to attend law school and participate in the hospital program because of her interest in women's issues in general and domestic violence in particular. Her family had sheltered a young woman (a friend of the family) who had left her husband, a man who had abused her physically and sexually. The husband had threatened suicide and also to harm Alexandra's family. Alexandra's mother had been involved with a domestic violence awareness group, which Alexandra also joined in high school. Alexandra had an aunt in an abusive relationship and had been in a controlling relationship herself.

+ Kathy, fifty-one, was a first-year law student who identified as white and Jewish. She had retired from a career in business and was going to law school because she was "interested in giving back and having a positive impact" on others' lives, although she wasn't sure what form that would take. She had been working for about a year as a court-appointed special advocate for children, and in that role, she had received training in domestic violence. She had no direct or secondhand experience with domestic violence.

The following students served as advocates at the court:

+ Talia, twenty-three, identified as white, of Middle Eastern descent, and not religious. Talia had participated in the hospital program the previous year and then had worked the following summer for the same hospital as a domestic violence advocate. As an undergraduate student, Talia had completed a medical internship in domestic violence in a hospital emergency department in New York. After graduating from college, she conducted research in the Middle East on women's access to health care. Talia chose

Northeastern University School of Law because of the DVI and its public interest focus.

+ Helen, twenty-six, identified as Asian American and not religious. Helen had participated in the hospital program as both an interviewer and a team leader (when she took part in my study of that program). Helen decided to attend law school because of her interest in women's rights and domestic violence and chose Northeastern because of the DVI. During law school, she worked for the family and probate court and with a domestic violence advocacy center.

+ Hannah, twenty-seven, identified as white and Jewish. She had participated the previous year in the hospital program and took part in my study of that program. After graduating from college, she had worked as a human rights accompanier in Central America and did intake for a legal aid office. She was motivated to attend law school and become involved with the DVI because of a desire to help people affected by violence. During law school, she worked on the US-Mexico border with two different immigrant advocacy groups.

+ Chloe, twenty-five, identified as African American. She was raised as a Jehovah's Witness. Like Talia, Chloe had participated in the hospital program and had worked subsequently for the same hospital as a domestic violence advocate. Chloe came to law school and Northeastern University School of Law specifically to study domestic violence advocacy. She was motivated to pursue the work because many women in her family, including her mother and grandmother, had experienced physical, emotional, or sexual abuse.

+ Samantha, twenty-six, identified as African American, a child of immigrants from the Caribbean, and Christian. She grew up in the neighborhood served by the court where she worked. Unlike the other four advocates, she did not participate in the hospital program. Before law school, she worked for several years in a district attorney's office, sometimes assisting victim witness advocates. She was motivated to attend law school by the desire to "give people a voice." She took part in the court clinic program partly because of her own experience in a long-term emotionally abusive relationship with a suicidal and violent man.

Notes

Introduction

1. Burke and Carroll, *Independent Review*; David Abel, Eric Moskowitz, and Todd Feathers, "Sox Broadcaster's Son Held in Slaying of His Girlfriend: Had Been Freed Day before, without Bail, despite Violent Past," *Boston Globe*, August 17, 2013.

2. Burke and Carroll, *Independent Review*, 15–16. According to a neighbor, Martel said she had promised Remy's family that she would not seek to extend the order. Eric Moskowitz, "For Jared Remy, Leniency Was the Rule until One Lethal Night," *Boston Globe*, March 23, 2014.

3. One literature review found that "between 30% and 70% of [restraining orders] are violated" and that "evidence from large scale and some smaller scale community studies [shows] that those who obtained a [restraining order] were at greater risk for physical victimization." Russell, "Protective Orders," 535–36.

4. Messing and Campbell, "Use of Lethality Assessment."

5. "Fatal Failure; Remy Case Sheds Light on Court's Role," *Telegram & Gazette* (Massachusetts), August 21, 2013, http://www.telegram.com/article/20130821/NEWS/308219986.

6. Mather, "What Do Clients Want?"

7. Southworth, "Lawyer-Client Decisionmaking," 112.

8. Alfieri, "Antinomies of Poverty Law"; López, *Rebellious Lawyering*; Lucie White, "Subordination, Rhetorical Survival Skills."

9. Buel, "Effective Assistance of Counsel," 296–302; Schneider, *Battered Women*, 75–86.

10. Royster and Kirsch, *Feminist Rhetorical Practices*, 97.

11. Keith and Mountford, "Mt. Oread Manifesto," 3.

12. See, for example, Fleming, "Rhetoric as a Course of Study"; Glenn, Lyday, and Sharer, eds., *Rhetorical Education in America*; Hauser, "Teaching Rhetoric"; Keith and Mountford, "Mt. Oread Manifesto."

13. Logan, "'To Get an Education,'" 48.

14. See, for example, Enoch, *Refiguring Rhetorical Education*; Glenn, "Rhetorical Education in America," x; Gold and Hobbs, *Educating the New Southern Woman*; Hollis, *Liberating Voices*; Johnson, *Gender and Rhetorical Space*; Logan, *Liberating Language*.

15. Smith et al., *Sexual Violence Survey*, 2, 118.

16. Hauser, "Teaching Rhetoric," 40; Walker, *Genuine Teachers*, 223.

17. Some scholars in rhetoric lament that contemporary education no longer focuses on producing rhetors (see, e.g., Hauser, "Teaching Rhetoric"). Composition studies (a field allied but not coterminous with rhetorical studies) has been the site of a related but mostly inverted debate, with some scholars arguing that composition studies has historically been *too* interested in producing students and not interested enough in writing itself (see, e.g., Dobrin, *Postcomposition*; Sanchez, *Function of Theory*). Like many of my colleagues, I believe that we can address questions of agency without subscribing to the modernist notion of the autonomous speaking subject (see, e.g., Campbell, "Agency"; Geisler, "Teaching the Post-Modern Rhetor"; Miller, "What Can Automation Tell Us?").

18. Mertz, *Language of Law School.*

19. Clark, "Tracing the Roots," 317.

20. Chase, "Origins of Modern Professional Education," 330.

21. Sullivan et al., *Educating Lawyers,* 5.

22. Sullivan et al., 2.

23. Mertz, *Language of Law School,* 5.

24. Mertz, 5. See also Mootz, "Task of Legal Education," 135.

25. Sullivan et al., *Educating Lawyers,* 121.

26. Hasian, Condit, and Lucaites, "Rhetorical Boundaries," 339.

27. Harding, "Introduction."

28. Haraway, "Situated Knowledges," 581.

29. Haraway, 589.

30. Detienne and Vernant, *Cunning Intelligence,* 3–4.

31. Hawhee, *Bodily Arts,* 48.

32. Hawhee, *Bodily Arts,* 146.

33. See, for example, Boyle and Dunn, "Teaching Law Students," 229; Dauphinais, "Valuing and Nurturing Multiple Intelligences," 34; Jacobson, "Primer on Learning Styles," 155.

34. In rhetorical studies and the allied field of composition studies, see, for example, Alexander, "Glenn Gould"; Buchanan, *Regendering Delivery*; Ceraso, "(Re)Educating the Senses"; Conquergood, "Rethinking Elocution"; Fountain, *Rhetoric in the Flesh*; Johnson, *Gender and Rhetorical Space*; Kates, "Embodied Rhetoric"; Mountford, *Gendered Pulpit*; Selfe, "Movement of Air"; Shipka, *Composition Made Whole.*

35. Halloran, "Writing History on the Landscape," 130.

36. Rhetoric and composition scholars interested in the places of writing include Gere, "Kitchen Tables"; Grego and Thompson, *Teaching/Writing in Thirdspaces*; Mauk, "Location, Location, Location"; Reynolds, "Composition's Imagined Geographies"; Welch, *Living Room.* Those interested in service learning, the experiential equivalent of clinical legal education (CLE) in rhetoric and composition, include Deans, *Writing Partnerships*; Deans, Roswell, and Wurr, *Writing and Community Engagement*; Flower, *Community Literacy*; Mathieu, *Tactics of Hope.*

37. Baker, "Beyond *MacCrate,*" 317.

38. Dewey, *Democracy and Education,* 167, emphasis in original.

39. Clark and Young, "Changing Places," 73.

40. Clark and Young, 85.

41. *Oxford English Dictionary Online,* s.v., "attitude," accessed August 13, 2017, http://www.oed.com.ezproxy.neu.edu/view/Entry/12876.

42. Burke, *Attitudes toward History,* 394.

43. Burke, *Grammar of Motives,* 14.

44. Burke, *Grammar of Motives,* 14, emphasis in original.

45. Burke, *Attitudes toward History,* 394.

46. Hawhee, *Moving Bodies,* 72.

47. Burke, *Grammar of Motives,* 236.

48. Burke and Carroll, *Independent Review,* 23.

49. "A Blueprint for Domestic Violence Homicide Prevention," Jane Doe Inc., August 26, 2013, http://www.janedoe.org/site/assets/docs/Learn_More/DV_Homicide/2013_JDI _Blueprint_dv_homicide_prevention.pdf.

50. "Blueprint for Domestic Violence."

51. Enos and Kanter, "Who's Listening?," 107.

52. Enos and Kanter, 107.

53. Royster, "First Voice You Hear," 40.

54. Ratcliffe, *Rhetorical Listening*, 18.

55. Ratcliffe, *Rhetorical Listening*, 1.

56. Enos and Kanter, "Who's Listening?," 86.

57. Monberg, "Listening for Legacies," 87.

58. Mertz, *Language of Law School*, 97–137; Kruse, "Beyond Cardboard Clients"; Sarat, "Lawyers and Clients"; Sullivan et al., *Educating Lawyers*.

59. Alfieri, "Against Practice"; Jacobs, "People from the Footnotes."

60. Susan Bryant and Jean Koh Peters have developed an approach to cross-cultural lawyering that has been widely adopted in clinical programs across the country. Bryant and Peters, "Five Habits"; Bryant, "Five Habits"; Peters, "Habit, Story, Delight." Scholars in rhetoric and composition may be interested to know that Bryant and Peters have recently incorporated into their framework Peter Elbow's methodology of "doubting and believing." Bryant, Millstein, and Shalleck, *Transforming the Education of Lawyers*, 364.

61. Anna D. Wilde, "Law School Settles Case of Sex Discrimination," *Harvard Crimson*, September 22, 1993, http://www.thecrimson.com/article/1993/9/22/law-school-settles-case-of-sex/.

62. Gordon, *Heroes of Their Own Lives*; Pleck, *Domestic Tyranny*.

63. Buel, "Pedagogy of Domestic Violence Law," 340; Kanter, Enos, and Dalton, "Northeastern's Domestic Violence Institute," 381; Schneider, *Battered Women*, 212.

64. Merryman, "Survey of Domestic Violence Programs," 384.

65. The American Bar Association maintains a directory of current public interest clinics, including those specializing in domestic violence, at https://apps.americanbar.org/legalservices/probono/lawschools/pi_pi_clinics.html.

66. Kanter, Enos, and Dalton, "Northeastern's Domestic Violence Institute," 361.

67. Kanter, Enos, and Dalton, 368.

68. The hospital program continued at another hospital, St. Elizabeth's Medical Center, for another two years, until Kanter's retirement in 2013.

69. The biggest change is that students now take on a more traditional role for attorneys, appearing for clients and speaking on their behalf in legal proceedings.

70. Kanter, *Domestic Violence Manual: 2009*, 23.

71. US Department of Justice, *Intimate Partner Violence*, 3.

72. Smith et al., *Sexual Violence Survey*, 2, 118.

73. Johnson, "Patriarchal Terrorism."

74. Dunn, *Judging Victims*, 5.

75. Dunn, *Judging Victims*, 96.

76. Dunn, "'Victims' and 'Survivors.'"

77. Dunn, "'Victims' and 'Survivors,'" 23.

78. Andrus, *Entextualizing Domestic Violence*, 5–6.

79. Andrus, 6.

80. Materials also discussed violence by women against men, including work by so-called family violence researchers, who argue that women are just as violent as men in intimate relationships. See, for example, Gelles, *Violent Home*, and Straus, "Victims and Aggressors." Family violence researchers tend to rely on self-reporting of violent behavior in the home, ignoring the contexts and severity of violence. See Melton and Sillito, "Role of Gender," for a summary and evaluation of the family violence perspective.

81. Kanter, *Domestic Violence Manual: 2009*; Kanter, *Domestic Violence Manual: 2009–2010*.

Chapter 1

1. Edward Lewis, "Wife Killed in Domestic Dispute, Police Say," *Times Leader*, September 28, 2013, http://timesleader.com/archive/302894/news-local-news-866270-wife-killed-in-domestic-dispute-police-say.

2. James Halpin, "Domestic Dispute Ends in Murder," *Citizens' Voice*, September 28, 2013, http://citizensvoice.com/news/domestic-dispute-ends-in-murder-1.1559830.

3. Mahoney, "Legal Images," 5–6.

4. Campbell et al., "Risk Factors for Femicide," 1092.

5. Halpin, "Domestic Dispute Ends in Murder."

6. The comments appeared after Halpin's article reporting Aiello's murder was published. See Halpin, "Domestic Dispute Ends in Murder."

7. Kolb, *Moral Wages*, 7.

8. The increasingly familiar admonition to "become your own advocate" in health care or employment indicates the presumption that advocacy is not something one normally does only for oneself.

9. Zompetti, "Role of Advocacy," 175.

10. Fortun, *Advocacy after Bhopal*, 16, 349.

11. Burke, *Rhetoric of Motives*, 146.

12. Greenidge, *Legal Procedure of Cicero's Time*, 148.

13. The role later became more active, with *advocati* developing cases and delivering speeches on behalf of someone else. Jonaitis and Žalėnienė, "Concept of the Bar," 302–3.

14. Kennedy, "Rhetoric of Advocacy," 419–21. Women, as well as some others (e.g., young boys, old men, slaves, and the condemned), were prevented from speaking for themselves by law, while others (e.g., someone wounded and dying at the time of a trial) were prevented by infirmity.

15. Gagarin, *Antiphon the Athenian*, 3.

16. Sprague, *Older Sophists*, 282.

17. Keller and Grontkowski, "Mind's Eye," 208–15.

18. Haraway, "Situated Knowledges," 581.

19. Haraway, 589.

20. Collins, *Black Feminist Thought*, 36.

21. hooks, *Feminist Theory*, xvii.

22. Royster, "First Voice You Hear," 32.

23. Alcoff, "Speaking for Others," 9.

24. See, for example, Behar and Gordon, *Women Writing Culture*; Clifford and Marcus, *Writing Culture*; Di Leonardo, *Gender at the Crossroads*; Marcus and Fischer, *Anthropology as Cultural Critique*; Mascia-Lees, Sharpe, and Cohen, "Postmodern Turn in Anthropology."

25. Alcoff, "Speaking for Others," 10.

26. See Alcoff, 6, for a summary of these arguments.

27. Spivak, "Can the Subaltern Speak?," 308.

28. Spivak, 295, emphasis added.

29. Alcoff, "Speaking for Others," 17.

30. Alcoff, 24.

31. Enos and Kanter, "Who's Listening?," 86–87.

32. Seligman, *High Citadel*, 44.

33. Sullivan et al., *Educating Lawyers*, 3.

34. López, "Training Future Lawyers," 307.

35. Kruse, "Beyond Cardboard Clients," 104.

36. Shalleck, "Constructions of the Client," 1731, 1733, 1735, 1736.

37. Mertz, *Language of Law School*; Sullivan et al., *Educating Lawyers*.

38. Bourdieu, "Force of Law," 833.

39. Bourdieu, *Theory of Practice*, 78.

40. Burke, *Grammar of Motives*, 245.

41. Barry, Dubin, and Joy, "Clinical Education," 6.

42. Rowe, "Legal Clinics," 606–7.

43. Reed, *Training for the Public Profession*, 278.

44. Reed, 281–86.

45. Frank, "Clinical Lawyer-School," 915. Readers might wonder if these early critics of legal education were influenced by John Dewey, whose turn-of-the-century work was central to the educational progressive movement. Although some contemporary legal scholars draw on Dewey's ideas (see, e.g., MacFarlane, "Look before You Leap"; Piomelli, "Democratic Roots"; Smith, "Clinical Programs"), those working in the early to mid-twentieth century do not. Legal scholar Paul Maharg argues that although there was an "encounter" between Dewey and Columbia University Law School that resulted in failed educational experiments, Dewey did not engage the literature on legal pedagogy. Maharg, *Transforming Legal Education*.

46. Schrag and Meltsner, *Clinical Legal Education*, 3. Barry, Dubin, and Joy argue that CLE didn't take hold in the first part of the twentieth century for a number of reasons: law schools were trying to differentiate themselves in the educational marketplace from apprenticeships, law schools lacked the money to fund more labor-intensive clinical programs, law school teachers at the time disagreed about the value of practical training, and the professional associations attempting to raise standards for law schools did not encourage clinical experiences. Barry, Dubin, and Joy, "Clinical Education," 8–9.

47. Kinoy, "Present Crisis," 3.

48. Kinoy, 6, 10.

49. Barry, Dubin, and Joy, "Clinical Education," 19–21.

50. Ethan Bronner, "Law Schools' Applications Fall as Costs Rise and Jobs Are Cut," *New York Times Late Edition*, January 31, 2013; David Segal, "Is Law School a Losing Game?," *New York Times Late Edition*, January 9, 2011; Elizabeth Olson and David Segal, "A Steep Slide in Law School Enrollment Accelerates," *New York Times Late Edition*, December 18, 2014; Gerry Shih, "Downturn Dims Prospects Even at Top Law Schools," *New York Times Late Edition*, August 26, 2009; Sullivan et al., *Educating Lawyers*.

51. American Bar Association, *Report and Recommendations*, 1, 3.

52. American Bar Association, *ABA Standards*, 16. ABA-approved law schools must require at least eighty-three credit hours total for a juris doctor degree. The ABA standards previously did not require an experiential component. The Clinical Legal Education Association had advocated for fifteen credit hours, arguing that all other professions (such as medicine, social work, and pharmacy) require students to spend at least 25 percent of their educational preparation in "supervised professional practice." Clinical Legal Education Association, *Comment*, 1.

53. Meltsner, "Celebrating *The Lawyering Process*," 327.

54. Kruse, "Fortress in the Sand," 371.

55. Binder et al., *Lawyers as Counselors*, 80–83.

56. Jacobs, "People from the Footnotes," 350.

57. Bryant, Milstein, and Shalleck, *Transforming the Education of Lawyers*.

58. See, for example, López, *Rebellious Lawyering*; Piomelli, "Democratic Roots of Collaborative Lawyering"; Piomelli, "Challenge of Democratic Lawyering"; Russell, "Entering Great America."

59. Kanter, Enos, and Dalton, "Northeastern's Domestic Violence Institute," 366.

60. Pleck, *Domestic Tyranny*, 4.

61. Pleck, 184–85.

62. Vaughan, "Last Refuge," 114.

63. Pleck, *Domestic Tyranny*, 191.

64. Schechter, *Women and Male Violence*, 251.

65. "Statement of Core Values," Jane Doe Inc., accessed August 3, 2017, http://www.jane
doe.org/who_we_are/jdis_members/core_values.

66. Kolb, *Moral Wages*, 53.

67. Kolb, 59.

68. Pence and Paymar, *Education Groups*, 2.

69. Burke and Carroll, *Independent Review*, 7.

70. Eric Moskowitz, "'I'm Planning My Escape,' Jennifer Martel Said," *Boston Globe*,
May 18, 2014.

71. Burke and Carroll, *Independent Review*, 9.

72. Enos and Kanter, "Who's Listening?," 95.

73. Kanter, Enos, and Dalton, "Northeastern's Domestic Violence Institute," 366.

74. Enos and Kanter, "Who's Listening?," 96.

75. Kanter, Enos, and Dalton, "Northeastern's Domestic Violence Institute," 366.

76. Kanter, Enos, and Dalton, 412n67.

77. Enos and Kanter, "Who's Listening?," 99.

78. Dunn and Powell-Williams, "'Everybody Makes Choices,'" 997.

79. Kolb, *Moral Wages*, 71.

80. Kolb, 71, 73, 80.

81. Enos and Kanter, "Who's Listening?," 85–86.

82. Mindes and Acock, "Trickster, Hero, Helper," 180, 204.

83. Menkel-Meadow, "Can They Do That?"

84. All names given to the students who participated in my study are pseudonyms.

85. Kanter, *Domestic Violence Manual: 2009*, 227, 170.

86. Kanter, *Domestic Violence Manual: 2009*, 185.

87. Enos and Kanter, "Who's Listening?," 93.

88. Enos and Kanter, 94.

Chapter 2

1. Enos and Kanter, "Who's Listening?," 98.

2. Enos and Kanter, 112.

3. The students were from Boston College, Boston University, Harvard University, New
England School of Law, Northeastern University, and Suffolk University.

4. Aristotle, *On Rhetoric*, 112.

5. Ratcliffe, *Anglo-American Feminist Challenges*, 20.

6. Ritchie and Ronald, "Introduction," xxiv.

7. See, for example, Hill, *Speaking Truth to Power*; Williams, *Alchemy of Race and Rights*.

8. Scheppele, "Just the Facts," 126.

9. "Help a Friend or Family Member," National Domestic Violence Hotline, accessed July
27, 2016, http://www.thehotline.org/help/help-for-friends-and-family.

10. "Get Help," National Coalition Against Domestic Violence, accessed April 29, 2016,
http://www.ncadv.org/need-help/get-help.

11. David E. Frank, "Longtime Remy Lawyer Peter Bella Responds to Criticisms," *Massachusetts Lawyers Weekly*, March 28, 2014, http://masslawyersweekly.com/2014/03/28/longtime-remy-lawyer-peter-bella-responds-to-criticisms/.

12. The hashtag #WhyIStayed was started by Beverly Gooden, who shared her own reasons for staying in an abusive relationship after reading tweets blaming Janay Rice. Gooden has since embarked on a speaking tour advocating for victims of domestic violence. Beverly Gooden, "Why We Stayed," *New York Times*, October 13, 2004, https://kristof.blogs.nytimes.com/2014/10/13/why-we-stayed/?_r=0.

13. Schutte, Malouff, and Doyle, "Returning to a Battering Relationship."

14. Baker, "And I Went Back."

15. Eric Moskowitz, "'I'm Planning My Escape,' Jennifer Martel Said," *Boston Globe*, May 18, 2014.

16. Bell et al., "Dynamics of Staying and Leaving"; Fleury et al., "Ending the Relationship."

17. Meyers, *News Coverage*.

18. See, for example, Goodmark, "Battered Woman"; Morrison, "Changing the Domestic Violence (Dis)Course"; Schneider, *Battered Women*.

19. Schuster and Propen, *Victim Advocacy in the Courtroom*, 88.

20. Andrus, *Entextualizing Domestic Violence*, 109.

21. Buel, "Pedagogy of Domestic Violence Law," 315.

22. In mid-eighteenth-century England, a man who killed his wife was treated as if he had killed an ordinary person, while a woman who killed her husband was regarded as having killed her sovereign and thus having committed treason, the penalty for which was to be "drawn and burnt alive." Blackstone, *Commentaries*, 444n32. Similarly, the provocation defense emerged in English common law during the seventeenth century to reduce a charge of murder to manslaughter when the defense could show that the accused was provoked by an event likely to make a "reasonable man" lose control. Ashworth, "Doctrine of Provocation," 292. In early American law, the provocation defense was explicitly gendered in some jurisdictions: men who killed after witnessing their wives in an adulterous act were committing justifiable homicide (i.e., were acquitted), while wives who killed their husbands in the same circumstances were guilty of murder. Yet even after these categories had been replaced by a supposedly gender-neutral standard of the "reasonable person," the provocation defense still favored men because women are less likely to kill in a moment of passion following their husbands' infidelity and because violence from men in those circumstances is viewed as a normal part of masculine behavior. Lee, *Murder and the Reasonable Man*, 7.

23. Schneider, *Battered Women*, 112–47.

24. Schneider, 119.

25. Walker, *Battered Woman Syndrome*; Goodmark, "Battered Woman"; Morrison, "Changing the Domestic Violence (Dis)Course."

26. Schneider, *Battered Women*, 125.

27. Walker, *Battered Woman Syndrome*, 69–84.

28. Allard, "Rethinking Battered Woman Syndrome," 197.

29. Ellen Goodman, "A Documentary about Terrorism—in the Home," *Boston Globe*, March 17, 1994.

30. Susan K. Howards, an attorney for Moore, the first to be released, coined the term "Framingham Eight" after the memory of the "Birmingham Four," the four African American girls killed in a church bombing in 1963. Francie Latour, "Happy Endings Elude the Framingham Eight; after Celebrity's Glare, They Run into New Walls," *Boston Globe*, February 15, 1998. Members of the Framingham Eight include Patricia Allen, Shannon Booker, Lisa

Grimshaw, Patricia Hennessy, Elaine Hyde, Eugenia Moore, Debra Reid, and Meekah Scott. All but one had killed men; Reid had killed her female partner. All but Patricia Hennessy were released early from prison. Buel, "Effective Assistance of Counsel," 322n672. *Defending Our Lives* features Booker, Grimshaw, Hennessy, and Moore (all still imprisoned at the time), as well as Scott (who was released pending appeal).

31. Frank Phillips, "Weld Relaxes Prison Appeal by Battered Women," *Boston Globe*, September 27, 1991.

32. "Defending Our Lives," *Cambridge Documentary Films*, last modified October 30, 2016, http://www.cambridgedocumentaryfilms.org/filmsPages/defending.html.

33. Bella English, "Soul Battered but Not Beaten," *Boston Globe*, March 15, 1995.

34. Vieira, "Framingham Eight."

35. Reynolds, *Ethos as Location*," 332.

36. Ratcliffe, *Rhetorical Listening*, 32–33.

37. Nichols, *Representing Reality*, 4.

38. Burke, *Rhetoric of Motives*, 20.

39. Ratcliffe, *Rhetorical Listening*, 32.

40. Burke, *Grammar of Motives*, 3–20.

41. Burke, "Dramatism," 446.

42. Burke, *Grammar of Motives*, 6–7.

43. Crusius, "Case for Kenneth Burke," 28.

44. Schechter, *Women and Male Violence*, 31–34.

45. Freeman, *Politics of Women's Liberation*.

46. Schneider, *Battered Women*, 59.

47. Schneider, 61–62, 136.

48. Ratcliffe, *Rhetorical Listening*, 98.

49. An attorney who represented one of the heterosexual members of the Framingham Eight in her commutation hearings came to believe that her own use of heteronormative language and standards when discussing domestic violence ultimately disadvantaged the lone lesbian in the group. Goldfarb, "Describing without Circumscribing."

50. Fleury et al., "Ending the Relationship."

51. Buel, "Effective Assistance of Counsel," 323.

52. Restuccia, *Melancholics in Love*, 94.

53. Vieira, "Framingham Eight."

54. Kunzelman, "Time for Healing."

55. Kanter, Enos, and Dalton, "Northeastern's Domestic Violence Institute," 366.

56. Kennedy, *Progymnasmata*, 45.

57. Kennedy, *Progymnasmata*, x.

58. D'Angelo, "Rhetoric of Ekphrasis," 440.

59. Perelman and Olbrechts-Tyteca, *New Rhetoric*, 51.

60. Sullivan, "Closer Look at Education," 71.

61. Fountain, *Rhetoric in the Flesh*, 20.

62. Kanter, *Interviewer/Advocate Manual*, 110.

63. Perelman and Olbrechts-Tyteca, *New Rhetoric*, 50.

Chapter 3

1. Enos and Kanter, "Who's Listening?," 102. The collaboration ended in 2011, after Boston Medical Center received funding for an in-house advocacy program.

2. "Population and Patient Profile Tables, Charts, and Statistics," Boston Medical Center, accessed August 10, 2016, http://www.bumc.bu.edu/crro/recruitment/resources/tables/; Mead et al., *Assessment of the Safety Net*, 10.

3. Enos and Kanter, "Who's Listening?," 102.

4. Kanter, *Interviewer/Advocate Manual*, 1.

5. Kanter, *Interviewer/Advocate Manual*, 29; Enos and Kanter, "Who's Listening?," 109.

6. For women accompanied by other adults, students were advised to ask for help from the medical staff to move them to the waiting room, "without mentioning the program as the reason." Kanter, *Interviewer/Advocate Manual: 2009–2010*, 29.

7. Kanter, *Interviewer/Advocate Manual*, 6.

8. Enos and Kanter, "Who's Listening?," 85.

9. Kanter, *Interviewer/Advocate Manual*, 6.

10. Alcoff, "Speaking for Others," 24.

11. Enos and Kanter, "Who's Listening?," 86.

12. Burke, "(Nonsymbolic) Motion," 816, emphasis in original.

13. Mountford, *Gendered Pulpit*, 17.

14. Dawood et al., "Estimated Global Mortality."

15. The stabbing occurred during a shift of the team that I was observing. Fortunately (and unfortunately) for me, I missed the shift because I had contracted H1N1. The stabbing was unique in the history of the program and caused great concern among students and faculty, but no students that I interviewed or observed dropped out of the program because of the incident.

16. Kanter, *Interviewer/Advocate Manual*, 25.

17. Enos and Kanter, "Who's Listening?," 114.

18. Mezirow, *Transformative Dimensions of Adult Learning*, 168.

19. Kanter, *Interviewer/Advocate Manual*, 56.

20. Mezirow, *Transformative Dimensions of Adult Learning*, 168.

21. Mezirow, 167.

22. Enos and Kanter, "Who's Listening?," 90.

23. Enos and Kanter, 108, 91.

24. Enos and Kanter, 96, 108.

25. Enos and Kanter, 90.

26. Enos and Kanter.

27. Mass. Gen. Laws ch. 209A. See the next chapter for a reproduction of the complaint form, which lists these requirements.

28. Sullivan et al., *Educating Lawyers*, 103.

29. Lubet, *Modern Trial Advocacy*, 8–9.

30. Goodmark, "Clinical Cognitive Dissonance," 316–17.

31. Kanter, *Interviewer/Advocate Manual*, 6.

32. Kanter, *Interviewer/Advocate Manual*, 31.

33. Kanter, *Interviewer/Advocate Manual*, 35–36.

34. Kanter, *Interviewer/Advocate Manual*, 132.

35. Kanter, *Interviewer/Advocate Manual*, 132.

36. Burke, *Rhetoric of Motives*, 20.

37. Ratcliffe, *Rhetorical Listening*, 100.

38. Ratcliffe, *Rhetorical Listening*, 72–73.

39. Ratcliffe, *Rhetorical Listening*, 62.

40. Ratcliffe, *Rhetorical Listening*, 73.

41. Ratcliffe, *Rhetorical Listening*, 73.

42. Ratcliffe, *Rhetorical Listening*, 33.

43. "Myths and Facts about Domestic Violence," Domestic Violence Intervention Program, accessed August 11, 2016, http://www.dvipiowa.org/myths-facts-about-domestic-violence/.

44. "Myths and Facts."

45. Kanter, *Interviewer/Advocate Manual*, 135.

46. Enos and Kanter, "Who's Listening?," 134.

47. Enos and Kanter, 134.

Chapter 4

1. DeJong and Burgess-Proctor, "Personal Protection Order Statutes."

2. Mass. Gen. Laws ch. 209A.

3. Advocates who support plaintiffs in abuse prevention order hearings are different from the victim witness advocates associated with prosecutors' offices. The latter are employed by the state to assist victims of crimes that are being prosecuted.

4. Burke and Carroll, *Independent Review*, 3. According to the review, victim witness advocates in the district attorney's office are "trained on [domestic violence] issues" but are not "specialized [domestic violence] advocates" (29).

5. Commonwealth of Massachusetts Trial Court, "Guidelines for Judicial Practice," 75.

6. After Lois Kanter retired, the court program shifted focus. Although still embracing a client empowerment philosophy, students in the court program beginning in 2013 took on a more traditional role for attorneys, often speaking for clients and appearing on their behalf.

7. Grabill, "On Being Useful," 204.

8. Grabill, 204.

9. Boston Redevelopment Authority, *Back Bay-Beacon*; Boston Redevelopment Authority, *Dorchester*; Boston Redevelopment Authority, *Roxbury*.

10. Crenshaw, "Mapping the Margins," 1245–49.

11. Reddick, Nelson, and Caulfield, "Racial and Gender Diversity," 30.

12. Ptacek, *Battered Women*, 51.

13. Eileen McNamara, "Judge Criticized after Woman's Death," *Boston Globe*, September 21, 1986.

14. Ptacek, *Battered Women*, 5.

15. Ptacek, 174–76.

16. Ptacek, 130.

17. Smart, *Feminism*, 4.

18. Smart, 10.

19. Naffine, *Law and the Sexes*, xii.

20. See, for example, Bell, *We Are Not Saved*; Delgado and Stefancic, *Critical Race Theory*; Harris, "Whiteness as Property"; Williams, *Seeing a Color-Blind Future*.

21. Ptacek, *Battered Women*, 125, 177.

22. Williams, *Alchemy of Race and Rights*, 56.

23. López, *Rebellious Lawyering*, 174.

24. Burke, *Rhetoric of Motives*, 21.

25. Kanter, Enos, and Dalton, "Northeastern's Domestic Violence Institute," 370.

26. López, "Training Future Lawyers," 323.

27. Kanter, *Domestic Violence Manual*, 23.

28. de Certeau, *Practice of Everyday Life*, 117.

29. de Certeau, emphasis in original.

30. Foucault, *History of Sexuality*, 94.

31. de Certeau, *Practice of Everyday Life*, 89.

32. López, *Rebellious Lawyering*, 62.

33. Hawhee, *Bodily Arts*, 58.

34. Hawhee, *Bodily Arts*, 128.

35. Hawhee, *Bodily Arts*, 128.

36. Hawhee, *Bodily Arts*, 68.

37. Hawhee, *Bodily Arts*, 148. Hawhee uses the word *opponents* to highlight the agonistic quality of ancient Greek culture. But *agonism* did not mean just the desire for victory in a competition. Instead, as Hawhee explains, *agon* at its root means "gathering," and *agonism* for the Greeks focused as much on the contest (gathering) itself as on the outcome. The *agon* served as an environment for "a productive training practice wherein subject production takes place through the encounter itself" (16).

38. de Certeau, *Practice of Everyday Life*, 83.

39. Murphy, "Roman Writing Instruction," 73, emphasis in original.

40. Kolb, *Moral Wages*, 118.

41. The two-page form is accompanied by a half page of instructions. Mass. Gen. Laws ch. 209A.

42. Daniels, "Invisible Work"; DeVault, *Feeding the Family*; Fletcher, *Disappearing Acts*; Hochschild, *Managed Heart*; Kolb, *Moral Wages*.

43. Ratcliffe, *Rhetorical Listening*, 99, emphasis in original.

44. Ratcliffe, *Rhetorical Listening*, 32.

45. Grabill, "On Being Useful," 205.

46. Although domestic violence can take many forms, including emotional, psychological, and financial, the Massachusetts law focuses on physical and sexual harm.

47. I have categorized these arguments using the ancient theory of stasis, attributed to Hermagoras of Temnos. Stasis theory was developed to help speakers identify the central point at issue in legal proceedings. The four stases are *fact* (whether something happened), *definition* (what sort of thing happened), *quality* (the nature of the thing that happened), and *policy* (what can be done). For a discussion of the relevance of stasis theory to modern legal argument, see Hohmann, "Dynamics of Stasis."

48. de Certeau, *Practice of Everyday Life*, xviii.

49. de Certeau, xviii.

50. Bourdieu, *Logic of Practice*, 66.

51. Schuster and Propen, *Victim Advocacy*, 126–27.

52. Resnik, "Asking about Gender," 957.

53. Ptacek, *Battered Women*, 148.

54. Commonwealth of Massachusetts Trial Court, "Guidelines for Judicial Practice," 70.

55. A couple of advocates also noted problems that male victims had with establishing credibility because of gendered ideas of victimhood. Chloe, who had a client with an abusive female partner, said that it "felt like the audience in the court were belittling [him]. You would hear snickers from people in the audience, people were laughing. I think it deals a lot with this idea in—I don't want to say black culture—but this ideal in our society that men are supposed to be strong and courageous, and to hear that they are being harassed or hurt or abused by a woman is funny to them." In this case, the man was feminized by the audience, seen as weak and therefore as unsympathetic.

56. Schuster and Propen, *Victim Advocacy*, 35, 88, 3.

57. Burke and Carroll, *Independent Review*, 6.

58. Schuster and Propen, *Victim Advocacy*, 37.

59. Schuster and Propen, 116, 123.

60. López, *Rebellious Lawyering*, 25.

61. Glenn, *Unspoken*, 2, emphasis in original.

62. Glenn, *Unspoken*, 7.

63. Schuster and Propen, *Victim Advocacy*, 90.

64. Kanter, *Domestic Violence Manual: 2009–10*, 168.

65. Kanter, *Domestic Violence Manual: 2009–10*, 169.

66. White, *Justice as Translation*, 260–61.

Conclusion

1. Bryant, Millstein, and Shalleck, *Transforming the Education of Lawyers*, 350.

2. Mertz, *Language of Law School*.

3. Williams, *Alchemy of Race and Rights*, 12, emphasis in original.

4. Williams, *Alchemy of Race and Rights*, 12–13.

5. An additional move that rounds out Ratcliffe's theory of rhetorical listening is "promoting an understanding of self and other." Ratcliffe, *Rhetorical Listening*, 26–33.

6. Scholars writing about rhetorical listening include contributors to Glenn and Ratcliffe, *Silence and Listening*; Monberg, "Listening for Legacies"; and Royster, "First Voice You Hear." Other methods of rhetorical criticism seem potentially powerful for helping law students see the situatedness of claims. They include Burke's pentadic criticism, Elbow's method of doubting and believing, Royster's idea of critical imagination, Royster and Kirsch's method of tacking in and out, and Toulmin's notion of argument warrants. Burke, *Grammar of Motives*; Elbow, *Writing without Teachers*; Royster, *Traces of a Stream*; Royster and Kirsch, *Feminist Rhetorical Practices*; Toulmin, *Uses of Argument*. (Elbow's strategy of doubting and believing is already used by clinical legal educators Susan Bryant and Jean Koh Peters. Bryant, Millstein, and Shalleck, *Transforming the Education of Lawyers*, 364.)

7. See Ambrose et al., *How Learning Works*, 127.

8. The prestige of moot court participation may vary across law schools and employers, especially when compared to participation on the editorial board of a law review.

9. Of course, silence can also signal deference to power. Glenn, *Unbroken*.

10. Hawhee, *Bodily Arts*, 148.

11. For example, advocacy for a patient's "rights, health, and safety" is explicitly named in the code of ethics of the American Nurses Association. "Code of Ethics for Nurses with Interpretive Statements," American Nurses Association, accessed July 21, 2017, http://nursing world.org/DocumentVault/Ethics-1/Code-of-Ethics-for-Nurses.html. How to teach advocacy to students is part of conversations in that field. See, for example, Krautscheid, "Embedding Microethical Dilemmas"; Snyder, "Emancipatory Knowing."

12. Both professions have an extensive literature in client or patient empowerment. In social work, for example, see Simon, *Empowerment Tradition*; in medicine, see Guadagnoli and Ward, "Patient Participation," and Castro et al., "Patient Empowerment."

13. For other calls to bring rhetoric into legal education, see, for example, Berger, "Studying and Teaching"; Hasian, Condit, and Lucaites, "Rhetorical Boundaries of 'The Law'"; Levine and Saunders, "Thinking like a Rhetor"; Maharg, *Transforming Legal Education*; Mootz, "Vico, Llewellyn,"; Scallen, "Evidence Law"; Wetlaufer, "Rhetoric and Its Denial"; White, *Expectation to Experience*; White, *Heracles' Bow*.

14. See, for example, Rieke and Stutman, *Communication in Legal Advocacy.* There is already recognition about the relevance of rhetoric and composition research and pedagogy to legal writing. See Sullivan et al., *Educating Lawyers,* 108, as well as *Legal Communication & Rhetoric,* the journal of the Association of Legal Writing Directors.

15. A notable exception is Rieke, "Rhetorical Theory in American Legal Practice," which traces rhetorical theory in the education of American lawyers from the colonial period to the mid-twentieth century. For an ethnographic study of a legal writing course, see Cauthen, *Black Letters.*

16. According to the American Bar Association's Model Rules of Professional Conduct, a lawyer is "a representative of clients, an officer of the legal system and a public citizen having special responsibility for the quality of justice." "Model Rules of Professional Conduct: Preamble and Scope," American Bar Association, accessed August 13, 2017, https://www.americanbar .org/groups/professional_responsibility/publications/model_rules_of_professional _conduct/model_rules_of_professional_conduct_preamble_scope.html.

17. Hauser, "Teaching Rhetoric," 52.

Appendix A

1. Both studies were approved by Northeastern University's Institutional Review Board (IRB #09-06-14 and #10-10-23). The hospital study was determined to be exempt by the Institutional Review Board at Boston Medical Center (Protocol #H-28571).

Bibliography

Alcoff, Linda. "The Problem of Speaking for Others." *Cultural Critique* 20 (1991–92): 5–32.

Alexander, Jonathan. "Glenn Gould and the Rhetorics of Sound." *Computers and Composition* 37 (2015): 73–89.

Alfieri, Anthony V. "Against Practice." *Michigan Law Review* 107, no. 6 (2009): 1073–92.

———. "The Antinomies of Poverty Law and a Theory of Dialogic Empowerment." *New York University Review of Law and Social Change* 16 (1987–88): 659–712.

Allard, Sharon Angella. "Rethinking Battered Woman Syndrome: A Black Feminist Perspective." *UCLA Women's Law Journal* 1 (1991): 191–207.

Ambrose, Susan A., Michael W. Bridges, Michele DiPietro, Marsha C. Lovett, and Marie K. Norman. *How Learning Works: Seven Research-Based Principles for Smart Teaching.* San Francisco: Jossey-Bass, 2010.

American Bar Association. *ABA Standards and Rules of Procedure for Approval of Law Schools, 2015–2016.* Chicago: American Bar Association, 2014. http://www.americanbar.org /content/dam/aba/publications/misc/legal_education/Standards/2014_2015_aba _standards_and_rules_of_procedure_for_approval_of_law_schools_bookmarked .authcheckdam.pdf.

———. Task Force on the Future of Legal Education. *Report and Recommendations.* Chicago: American Bar Association, January 2014. http://www.americanbar.org/content/dam /aba/administrative/professional_responsibility/report_and_recommendations_of _aba_task_force.authcheckdam.pdf.

Andrus, Jennifer. *Entextualizing Domestic Violence: Language Ideology and Violence against Women in the Anglo-American Hearsay Principle.* Oxford: Oxford University Press, 2015.

Aristotle. *On Rhetoric: A Theory of Civic Discourse.* 2nd ed. Translated by George A. Kennedy. Oxford: Oxford University Press, 2007.

Ashworth, Andrew J. "The Doctrine of Provocation." *Cambridge Law Journal* 35, no. 2 (1976), 292–320.

Baker, Brook K. "Beyond *MacCrate*: The Role of Context, Experience, Theory, and Reflection in Ecological Learning." *Arizona Law Review* 36 (1994): 287–356.

Baker, Phyllis L. "And I Went Back: Battered Women's Negotiation of Choice." *Journal of Contemporary Ethnography* 26, no. 1 (1997): 55–75.

Barry, Margaret Martin, Jon C. Dubin, and Peter A. Joy. "Clinical Education for This Millennium: The Third Wave." *Clinical Law Review* 7 (2000–2001): 1–75.

Behar, Ruth, and Deborah A. Gordon, eds. *Women Writing Culture.* Berkeley: University of California Press, 1995.

Bell, Derrick A. *And We Are Not Saved: The Elusive Quest for Racial Justice.* New York: Basic Books, 1987.

Bell, Margaret E., Lisa A. Goodman, and Mary Ann Dutton. "The Dynamics of Staying and Leaving: Implications for Battered Women's Emotional Well-Being and Experiences of Violence at the End of a Year." *Journal of Family Violence* 22, no. 6 (2007): 413–28.

Berger, Linda L. "Studying and Teaching 'Law as Rhetoric': A Place to Stand." *Legal Writing: The Journal of the Legal Writing Institute* 16 (2010): 3–64.

Binder, David A., Paul Bergman, Paul R. Tremblay, and Ian S. Weinstein. *Lawyers as Counselors: A Client-Centered Approach*. 3rd ed. St. Paul, MN: West Academic, 2011.

Binder, David, and Susan Price. *Legal Interviewing and Counseling: A Client-Centered Approach*. St. Paul, MN: West Academic, 1977.

Blackstone, William, with Thomas M. Cooley. *Commentaries on the Laws of England in Four Books*. Vol. 1, 3rd rev. ed. Chicago: Callaghan, 1884.

Boston Redevelopment Authority. BRA Research Division. *American Community Survey: 2007–2011 Estimate Back Bay-Beacon Neighborhood*, by Mark Melnik, Lingshan Gao, Alexis Kalevich, and Joanne Wong. May 2013. http://www.bostonplans.org/getattachment/b7046f35-4355-41e3-8e98-a30a3e5af338.

———. BRA Research Division. *American Community Survey: 2007–2011 Estimate Dorchester Neighborhood*, by Mark Melnik, Lingshan Gao, Alexis Kalevich, and Joanne Wong. May 2013. https://www.bostonplans.org/getattachment/1dad5a10-3597-4e03-a1b6-64e26cb20e1c.

———. BRA Research Division. *American Community Survey: 2007–2011 Estimate Roxbury Neighborhood*, by Mark Melnik, Lingshan Gao, Alexis Kalevich, and Joanne Wong. May 2013. https://www.bostonplans.org/getattachment/81f70f74-4574-4106-934d-775e50ac9bcd.

Bourdieu, Pierre. "The Force of Law: Toward a Sociology of the Juridical Field." *Hastings Law Journal* 38 (1986–87): 805–53.

———. *The Logic of Practice*. Stanford: Stanford University Press, 1990.

———. *Outline of a Theory of Practice*. Cambridge: Cambridge University Press, 1977.

Boyle, Robin A., and Rita Dunn. "Teaching Law Students through Individual Learning Styles." *Albany Law Review* 62 (1998): 213–55.

Bryant, Susan. "The Five Habits: Building Cross-Cultural Competence in Lawyers." *Clinical Law Review* 8 (2001): 33–107.

Bryant, Susan, Elliott S. Milstein, and Ann C. Shalleck. *Transforming the Education of Lawyers: The Theory and Practice of Clinical Pedagogy*. Durham: Carolina Academic, 2014.

Bryant, Susan, and Jean Koh Peters. "Five Habits for Cross-Cultural Lawyering." In *Race, Culture, Psychology, and Law*, edited by Kimberly Holt Barrett and William H. George, 47–62. Thousand Oaks, CA: Sage, 2005.

Buchanan, Lindal. *Regendering Delivery: The Fifth Canon and Antebellum Women Rhetors*. Carbondale: Southern Illinois University Press, 2005.

Buel, Sarah M. "Effective Assistance of Counsel for Battered Women Defendants: A Normative Construct." *Harvard Women's Law Journal* 26 (2003): 217–350.

———. "The Pedagogy of Domestic Violence Law: Situating Domestic Violence Work in Law Schools, Adding the Lenses of Race and Class." *American University Journal of Gender, Social Policy & the Law* 11, no. 2 (2003): 309–53.

Burke, Kenneth. *Attitudes toward History*. 3rd ed. Berkeley: University of California Press, 1984.

———. "Dramatism." In *International Encyclopedia of the Social Sciences*. Vol. 7, edited by David L. Sills, 445–47. New York: Crowell Collier and MacMillan, 1968.

———. *A Grammar of Motives*. Berkeley: University of California Press, 1969.

———. "(Nonsymbolic) Motion / (Symbolic) Action." *Critical Inquiry* 4, no. 4 (1978): 809–38.

———. *A Rhetoric of Motives*. Berkeley: University of California Press, 1950.

Burke, Kevin M., and Jeanmarie Carroll. *Independent Review of the Middlesex District Attorney's Office*. Commissioned by Middlesex District Attorney Marian T. Ryan. December 13, 2013. Accessed May 21, 2017. http://www.bostonglobe.com/metro/2014/08/21

/district-attorney-withheld-pages-remy-report/4kXpGvU6Ww0A30dHWrtezM
/igraphic.html?p1=Article_Related.

Campbell, Jacquelyn, Daniel Webster, Jane Koziol-McLain, Carolyn Block, Doris Campbell, Mary Ann Curry, Faye Gary, Nancy Glass, Judith McFarlane, Carolyn Sachs, Phyllis Sharps, Yvonne Ulrich, Susan A. Wilt, Jennifer Manganello, Xiao Xu, Janet Schollenberger, Victoria Frye, and Kathryn Laughon. "Risk Factors for Femicide in Abusive Relationships: Results from a Multisite Case Control Study." *American Journal of Public Health* 93, no. 7 (2003): 1089–97.

Campbell, Karlyn Kohrs. "Agency: Promiscuous and Protean." *Communication and Critical/ Cultural Studies* 2, no. 1 (2005): 1–19.

Castro, Eva Marie, Tine Van Regenmortel, Kris Vanhaecht, Walter Sermeus, and Ann Van Hecke. "Patient Empowerment, Patient Participation and Patient-Centeredness in Hospital Care: A Concept Analysis Based on a Literature Review." *Patient Education and Counseling* 99 (2016): 1923–39.

Cauthen, Randy. *Black Letters: An Ethnography of a Beginning Legal Writing Course.* Cresskill, NJ: Hampton Press, 2010.

Ceraso, Steph. "(Re)Educating the Senses: Multimodal Listening, Bodily Learning, and the Composition of Sonic Experiences." *College English* 77, no. 2 (2014): 102–23.

Chase, Anthony. "Origins of Modern Professional Education: The Harvard Case Method Conceived as Clinical Instruction in Law." *Nova Law Journal* 5 (1981): 323–63.

Clark, Caroline, and Morris Young. "Changing Places: Theorizing Space and Power Dynamics in Service-Learning." In *Service-Learning in Higher Education: Critical Issues and Directions,* edited by Dan W. Butin, 71–87. Gordonsville, VA: Palgrave Macmillan, 2005.

Clark, David S. "Tracing the Roots of American Legal Education: A Nineteenth-Century German Connection." *Rabel Journal of Comparative and International Private Law* 51 (1987): 313–33.

Clifford, James, and George E. Marcus, eds. *Writing Culture: The Poetics and Politics of Ethnography.* Berkeley: University of California Press, 1986.

Clinical Legal Education Association. *Comment of Clinical Legal Education Association on Proposed Standard 303.* New York: Clinical Legal Education Association, January 30, 2014. http://www.cleaweb.org/Resources/Documents/2014-01-14%20CLEA%20Chapter %203%20comment.pdf.

Collins, Patricia Hill. *Black Feminist Thought: Knowledge, Consciousness, and the Politics of Empowerment.* 2nd ed. New York: Routledge, 2000.

Commonwealth of Massachusetts Trial Court. "Guidelines for Judicial Practice: Abuse Prevention Proceedings." Last modified September 2011. http://www.mass.gov/courts /docs/209a/guidelines-2011.pdf.

Conquergood, Dwight. "Rethinking Elocution: The Trope of the Talking Book and Other Figures of Speech." *Text and Performance Quarterly* 20, no. 4 (2000): 325–41.

Crenshaw, Kimberlé. "Mapping the Margins: Intersectionality, Identity Politics, and Violence against Women of Color." *Stanford Law Review* 43, no. 6 (1991): 1241–99.

Crusius, Tim. "A Case for Kenneth Burke's Dialectic and Rhetoric." *Philosophy and Rhetoric* 19, no. 1 (1986): 23–37.

D'Angelo, Frank J. "The Rhetoric of Ekphrasis." *JAC: A Journal of Composition Theory* 18, no. 3 (1998): 439–47.

Daniels, Arlene Kaplan. "Invisible Work." *Social Problems* 34, no. 5 (1987): 403–15.

Dauphinais, Kirsten A. "Valuing and Nurturing Multiple Intelligences in Legal Education: A Paradigm Shift." *Washington and Lee Race and Ethnic Ancestry Law Journal* 11, no. 1 (2005): 1–42.

Dawood, Fatima S., A. Danielle Iuliano, Carrie Reed, Martin I. Meltzer, David K. Shay, Po-Yung Cheng, Don Bandaranayake, Robert F. Breiman, W. Abdullah Brooks, Philippe Buchy, Daniel R. Feikin, Karen B. Fowler, Aubree Gordon, Nguyen Tran Hien, Peter Horby, Q. Sue Huang, Mark A. Katz, Anand Krishnan, Renu Lal, Joel M. Montgomery, Kåre Mølbak, Richard Pebody, Anne M. Presanis, Hugo Razuri, Anneke Steens, Yeny O. Tinoco, Jacco Wallinga, Hongjie Yu, Sirenda Vong, Joseph Bresee, and Marc-Alan Widdowson. "Estimated Global Mortality Associated with the First 12 Months of 2009 Pandemic Influence A H1N1 Virus Circulation: A Modeling Study." *Lancet* 12, no. 9 (2012): 687–89.

Deans, Thomas. *Writing Partnerships: Service-Learning in Composition.* Urbana: National Council of Teachers of English, 2000.

Deans, Thomas, Barbara Roswell, and Adrian J. Wurr, eds. *Writing and Community Engagement: A Critical Sourcebook.* Boston: Bedford, 2010.

de Certeau, Michel. *The Practice of Everyday Life.* Translated by Steven Rendall. Berkeley: University of California Press, 1984.

Defending Our Lives. Directed by Margaret Lazarus and Renner Wunderlich. Cambridge, MA: Cambridge Documentary Films, 1993. DVD.

DeJong, Christina, and Amanda Burgess-Proctor. "A Summary of Personal Protection Order Statutes in the United States." *Violence against Women* 12, no. 1 (2006): 68–88.

Delgado, Richard, and Jean Stefancic. *Critical Race Theory: An Introduction.* New York: New York University Press, 2001.

Detienne, Marcel, and Jean-Pierre Vernant. *Cunning Intelligence in Greek Culture and Society.* Chicago: University of Chicago Press, 1991.

DeVault, Marjorie L. *Feeding the Family: The Social Organization of Caring as Gendered Work.* Chicago: University of Chicago Press, 1991.

Dewey, John. *Democracy and Education: An Introduction to the Philosophy of Education.* New York: Macmillan, 1922.

Di Leonardo, Micaela, ed. *Gender at the Crossroads of Knowledge: Feminist Anthropology in the Postmodern Era.* Berkeley: University of California Press, 1991.

Dobrin, Sidney I. *Postcomposition.* Carbondale: Southern Illinois University Press, 2011.

Dunn, Jennifer L. *Judging Victims: Why We Stigmatize Survivors and How They Reclaim Respect.* Boulder, CO: Lynne Rienner, 2010.

———. "'Victims' and 'Survivors': Emerging Vocabularies of Motive for 'Battered Women Who Stay.'" *Sociological Inquiry* 75, no. 1 (2005): 1–30.

Dunn, Jennifer L., and Melissa Powell-Williams. "'Everybody Makes Choices': Victim Advocates and the Social Construction of Battered Women's Victimization and Agency." *Violence against Women* 13, no. 10 (2007): 977–1001.

Elbow, Peter. *Writing without Teachers.* 2nd ed. Oxford: Oxford University Press, 1998.

Emerson, Robert M., Rachel I. Fretz, and Linda L. Shaw. *Writing Ethnographic Fieldnotes.* Chicago: University of Chicago Press, 1995.

Enoch, Jessica. *Refiguring Rhetorical Education: Women Teaching African American, Native American, and Chicano/a Students, 1865–1911.* Carbondale: Southern Illinois University Press, 2008.

Enos, V. Pualani, and Lois H. Kanter. "Who's Listening? Introducing Students to Client-Centered, Client-Empowering, and Multidisciplinary Problem-Solving in a Clinical Setting." *Clinical Law Review* 83 (2002–3): 83–134.

Fleming, David. "Rhetoric as a Course of Study." *College English* 61, no. 2 (1998): 169–91.

Fletcher, Joyce K. *Disappearing Acts: Gender, Power, and Relational Practice at Work.* Cambridge: Massachusetts Institute of Technology Press, 2001.

Fleury, Ruth E., Cris M. Sullivan, and Deborah I. Bybee. "When Ending the Relationship Does Not End the Violence: Women's Experiences of Violence by Former Partners." *Violence against Women* 6, no. 12 (2000), 1363–83.

Flower, Linda. *Community Literacy and the Rhetoric of Public Engagement.* Carbondale: Southern Illinois University Press, 2008.

Fortun, Kim. *Advocacy after Bhopal: Environmentalism, Disaster, New Global Orders.* Chicago: University of Chicago Press, 2001.

Foucault, Michel. *The History of Sexuality.* Vol. 1, *An Introduction.* New York: Vintage, 1990.

Fountain, T. Kenny. *Rhetoric in the Flesh: Trained Vision, Technical Expertise, and the Gross Anatomy Lab.* New York: Routledge, 2014.

Frank, Jerome. "Why Not a Clinical Lawyer-School?" *University of Pennsylvania Law Review* 81, no. 8 (1933): 907–23.

Freeman, Jo. *The Politics of Women's Liberation: A Case Study of an Emerging Social Movement and Its Relation to the Policy Process.* New York: David McKay, 1975.

Gagarin, Michael. *Antiphon the Athenian: Oratory, Law and Justice in the Age of the Sophists.* Austin: University of Texas Press, 2009.

Geisler, Cheryl. "Teaching the Post-Modern Rhetor: Continuing the Conversation on Rhetorical Agency." *Rhetoric Society Quarterly* 35, no. 4 (2005): 107–13.

Gelles, Richard J. *The Violent Home: A Study of Violent Aggression between Husbands and Wives.* Beverly Hills, CA: Sage, 1974.

Gere, Anne Ruggles. "Kitchen Tables and Rented Rooms: The Extracurricular of Composition." *College Composition and Communication* 45, no. 1 (1994): 75–92.

Glenn, Cheryl. "Rhetorical Education in America (A Broad Stroke Introduction)." In *Rhetorical Education in America,* edited by Cheryl Glenn, Margaret M. Lyday, and Wendy B. Sharer, vii–xvi. Tuscaloosa: University of Alabama Press, 2004.

———. *Unspoken: A Rhetoric of Silence.* Carbondale: Southern Illinois University Press, 2004.

Glenn, Cheryl, and Krista Ratcliffe, eds. *Silence and Listening as Rhetorical Arts.* Carbondale: Southern Illinois University Press, 2011.

Glenn, Cheryl, Margaret M. Lyday, and Wendy B. Sharer, eds. *Rhetorical Education in America.* Tuscaloosa: University of Alabama Press, 2004.

Gold, David, and Catherine L. Hobbs. *Educating the New Southern Woman: Speech, Writing, and Race at the Public Women's Colleges, 1884–1945.* Carbondale: Southern Illinois University Press, 2014.

Goldfarb, Phyllis. "Describing without Circumscribing: Questioning the Construction of Gender in the Discourse of Intimate Violence." *George Washington Law Review* 64 (1995): 582–631.

Goodmark, Leigh. "Clinical Cognitive Dissonance: The Values and Goals of Domestic Violence Clinics, the Legal System, and the Students Caught in the Middle." *Journal of Law and Policy* 20, no. 2 (2012): 301–23.

———. "When Is a Battered Woman Not a Battered Woman? When She Fights Back." *Yale Journal of Law and Feminism* 20 (2008): 75–129.

Gordon, Linda. *Heroes of Their Own Lives: The Politics and History of Family Violence, Boston 1880–1960.* New York: Viking Press, 1988.

Grabill, Jeff. "On Being Useful: Rhetoric and the Work of Engagement." In *The Public Work of Rhetoric: Citizen-Scholars and Civic Engagement,* edited by John M. Ackerman and David J. Coogan, 193–208. Columbia: University of South Carolina Press, 2010.

Greenidge, Abel Hendy Jones. *The Legal Procedure of Cicero's Time.* London: Clarendon Press, 1901.

Grego, Rhonda C., and Nancy S. Thompson. *Teaching/Writing in Thirdspaces: The Studio Approach*. Carbondale: Southern Illinois University Press, 2008.

Guadagnoli, Edward, and Patricia Ward. "Patient Participation in Decision-Making." *Social Science and Medicine* 47, no. 3 (1998): 329–39.

Halloran, S. Michael. "Writing History on the Landscape: The Tour Road at the Saratoga Battlefield as Text." In *Rhetorical Education in America*, edited by Cheryl Glenn, Margaret M. Lyday, and Wendy B. Sharer, 129–44. Tuscaloosa: University of Alabama Press, 2004.

Haraway, Donna. "Situated Knowledges: The Science Question in Feminism and the Privilege of Partial Perspective." *Feminist Studies* 14, no. 3 (1988): 575–99.

Harding, Sandra. "Introduction: Standpoint Theory as a Site of Political, Philosophical, and Scientific Debate." In *The Feminist Standpoint Reader: Intellectual and Political Controversies*, edited by Sandra Harding, 1–15. New York: Routledge, 2004.

Harris, Cheryl I. "Whiteness as Property." *Harvard Law Review* 106, no. 8 (1993): 1709–91.

Hasian, Marouf, Jr., Celeste Michelle Condit, and John Louis Lucaites. "The Rhetorical Boundaries of 'The Law': A Consideration of the Rhetorical Culture of Legal Practice and the Case of the 'Separate but Equal' Doctrine." *Quarterly Journal of Speech* 82 (1996); 323–42.

Hauser, Gerard A. "Teaching Rhetoric: Or Why Rhetoric Isn't Just Another Kind of Philosophy or Literary Criticism." *Rhetoric Society Quarterly* 34, no. 3 (2004): 39–53.

Hawhee, Debra. *Bodily Arts: Rhetoric and Athletics in Ancient Greece*. Austin: University of Texas Press, 2004.

———. *Moving Bodies: Kenneth Burke at the Edges of Language*. Columbia: University of South Carolina Press, 2009.

Hill, Anita. *Speaking Truth to Power*. New York: Doubleday, 1997.

Hochschild, Arlie Russell. *The Managed Heart: Commercialization of Human Feeling*. Berkeley: University of California Press, 1983.

Hohmann, Hanns. "The Dynamics of Stasis: Classical Rhetorical Theory and Modern Legal Argumentation." *American Journal of Jurisprudence* 34 (1989): 171–97.

Hollis, Karyn L. *Liberating Voices: Writing at the Bryn Mawr Summer School of Women Workers*. Carbondale: Southern Illinois University Press, 2004.

hooks, bell. *Feminist Theory: From Margin to Center*. New ed. New York: Routledge, 2015.

Jacobs, Michelle S. "People from the Footnotes: The Missing Element in Client-Centered Counseling." *Golden Gate University Law Review* 27 (1997): 345–422.

Jacobson, M. H. Sam, "A Primer on Learning Styles: Reaching Every Student." *Seattle University Law Review* 25 (2001): 139–77.

Jasinski, James. *Sourcebook on Rhetoric: Key Concepts in Contemporary Rhetorical Studies*. Thousand Oaks, CA: Sage, 2001.

Johnson, Michael P. "Patriarchal Terrorism and Common Couple Violence: Two Forms of Violence against Women." *Journal of Marriage and Family* 57, no. 2 (1995): 283–94.

Johnson, Nan. *Gender and Rhetorical Space in American Life, 1866–1920*. Carbondale: Southern Illinois University Press, 2002.

Jonaitis, Marius, and Inga Žalėnienė. "The Concept of the Bar and Fundamental Principles of an Advocate's Activity in Roman Law." *Jurisprudencija/Jurisprudence* 3 (2009): 299–312.

Kanter, Lois H., ed. *Domestic Violence Manual: 2009*. Vol. 1, *The Dynamics of Domestic Violence and Basic Advocacy Skills*. Boston: Northeastern University School of Law Domestic Violence Institute, 2009.

———, ed. *Domestic Violence Manual: 2009–2010*. Vol. 2, *Legal Advocacy for Battered Women in the District and Municipal Courts of Massachusetts*. Boston: Northeastern University School of Law Domestic Violence Institute, 2009.

———, ed. *Interviewer/Advocate Manual: 2009–2010*. Boston: Northeastern University School of Law Domestic Violence Institute, 2009.

Kanter, Lois H., V. Pualani Enos, and Clare Dalton. "Northeastern's Domestic Violence Institute: The Law School Clinic as an Integral Partner in a Coordinated Community Response to Domestic Violence." *Loyola Law Review* 47 (2001): 359–413.

Kates, Susan. "The Embodied Rhetoric of Hallie Quinn Brown." *College English* 59, no. 1 (1997): 59–71.

Keith, William, and Roxanne Mountford. "The Mt. Oread Manifesto on Rhetorical Education 2013." *Rhetoric Society Quarterly* 44, no. 1 (2014): 1–5.

Keller, Evelyn Fox, and Christine Grontkowski. "The Mind's Eye." In *Discovering Reality: Feminist Perspectives on Epistemology, Metaphysics, Methodology, and Philosophy of Science*, edited by Sandra Harding and Merrill B. Hintikka, 207–24. Dordrecht: Kluwer Academic, 1983.

Kennedy, George A., trans. *Progymnasmata: Greek Textbooks of Prose Composition and Rhetoric*. Leiden: Brill, 2003.

———. "The Rhetoric of Advocacy in Greece and Rome." *American Journal of Philology* 89, no. 4 (1968): 419–36.

Kinoy, Arthur. "The Present Crisis in American Legal Education." *Rutgers Law Review* 24 (1969–70): 1–10.

Kolb, Kenneth H. *Moral Wages: The Emotional Dilemmas of Victim Advocacy and Counseling*. Berkeley: University of California Press, 2014.

Krautscheid, Lorretta C. "Embedding Microethical Dilemmas in High-Fidelity Simulation Scenarios: Preparing Nursing Students for Ethical Practice." *Journal of Nursing Education* 56, no. 1 (2017): 55–58.

Kruse, Katherine R. "Beyond Cardboard Clients in Legal Ethics." *Georgetown Journal of Legal Ethics* 23 (2010): 103–54.

———. "Fortress in the Sand: The Plural Values of Client-Centered Representation." *Clinical Law Review* 12 (2006): 369–440.

Kunzelman, Michael. "Time for Healing: Struggling of the Framingham Eight Recalled after 10 Years of Freedom." *Dedham Transcript* (Dedham, MA), December 18, 2004.

Lee, Cynthia. *Murder and the Reasonable Man: Passion and Fear in the Criminal Courtroom*. New York: New York University Press, 2003.

Levine, Linda, and Kurt M. Saunders. "Thinking like a Rhetor." *Journal of Legal Education* 43 (1993): 108–22.

Littlejohn, Stephen W., and Karen A. Foss, eds. *Encyclopedia of Communication Theory*. Thousand Oaks, CA: Sage, 2009.

Logan, Shirley Wilson. *Liberating Language: Sites of Rhetorical Education in Nineteenth-Century Black America*. Carbondale: Southern Illinois University Press, 2008.

———. "'To Get an Education and Teach My People': Rhetoric for Social Change." In *Rhetorical Education in America*, edited by Cheryl Glenn, Margaret M. Lyday, and Wendy B. Sharer, 36–52. Tuscaloosa: University of Alabama Press, 2004.

López, Gerald P. *Rebellious Lawyering: One Chicano's Vision of Progressive Law Practice*. Boulder, CO: Westview Press, 1992.

———. "Training Future Lawyers to Work with the Politically and Socially Subordinated: Anti-Generic Legal Education." *West Virginia Law Review* 91 (1988–89): 305–87.

Lubet, Steven. *Modern Trial Advocacy: Analysis and Practice*. 3rd ed. South Bend, IN: National Institute for Trial Advocacy, 2004.

MacFarlane, Julie. "Look before You Leap: Knowledge and Learning in Legal Skills Education." *Journal of Law and Society* 19, no. 3 (1992): 293–319.

Maharg, Paul. *Transforming Legal Education: Learning and Teaching the Law in the Early Twenty-First Century*. Aldershot, UK: Ashgate, 2007.

Mahoney, Martha R. "Legal Images of Battered Women: Redefining the Issue of Separation." *Michigan Law Review* 90 (1991–92): 1–94.

Marcus, George E., and Michael M. J. Fischer. *Anthropology as Cultural Critique: An Experimental Moment in the Human Sciences*. Chicago: University of Chicago Press, 1996.

Mascia-Lees, Frances E., Patricia Sharpe, and Colleen Ballerino Cohen. "The Postmodern Turn in Anthropology: Cautions from a Feminist Perspective." *Signs* 15, no. 1 (1989): 7–33.

Mass. Gen. Laws ch. 209A.

Mather, Lynn. "What Do Clients Want? What Do Lawyers Do?" *Emory Law Journal* 52 (2003): 1066–86.

Mathieu, Paula. *Tactics of Hope: The Public Turn in English Composition*. Portsmouth, NH: Heinemann, 2005.

Mauk, Johnathon. "Location, Location, Location: The 'Real' (E)states of Being, Writing, and Thinking in Composition." *College English* 65, no. 4 (2003): 368–88.

Mead, Holly, Peter Shin, Marsha Regenstein, Kyle Kenney, and Karen Jones. *An Assessment of the Safety Net in Boston, Massachusetts*. Washington, DC: George Washington University Medical Center, School of Public Health and Health Services, Department of Health Policy, March 2004. Accessed August 10, 2016. http://hsrc.himmelfarb.gwu.edu/sphhs_policy_facpubs/186/.

Melton, Heather C., and Carrie Lefeve Sillito. "The Role of Gender in Officially Reported Intimate Partner Abuse." *Journal of Interpersonal Violence* 27, no. 6 (2012): 1090–1111.

Meltsner, Michael. "Celebrating *The Lawyering Process*." *Clinical Law Review* 10 (2003–4): 327–47.

Menkel-Meadow, Carrie. "Can They Do That? Legal Ethics in Popular Culture: Of Characters and Acts." *UCLA Law Review* 48 (2000–2001): 1305–37.

Merryman, Mithra. "A Survey of Domestic Violence Programs in Legal Education." *New England Law Review* 28 (1993): 383–452.

Mertz, Elizabeth. *The Language of Law School: Learning to "Think like a Lawyer."* Oxford: Oxford University Press, 2007.

Messing, Jill, and Jacquelyn Campbell. "The Use of Lethality Assessment in Domestic Violence Cases." *Family & Intimate Partner Violence Quarterly* 9, no. 1 (2016): 7–12.

Meyers, Marian. *News Coverage of Violence against Women: Engendering Blame*. Thousand Oaks, CA: Sage, 1997.

Mezirow, Jack. *Transformative Dimensions of Adult Learning*. San Francisco: Jossey-Bass, 1991.

Miller, Carolyn. "What Can Automation Tell Us about Agency?" *Rhetoric Society Quarterly* 37, no. 2 (2007): 137–57.

Mindes, Marvin W., and Alan C. Acock. "Trickster, Hero, Helper: A Report on the Lawyer Image." *American Bar Foundation Research Journal* 7, no. 1 (1982): 177–233.

Monberg, Terese Guinsatao. "Listening for Legacies: Or, How I Began to Hear Dorothy Laigo Cordova, the Pinay behind the Podium Known as FANHS." In *Representations: Doing Asian American Rhetoric*, edited by LuMing Mao and Morris Young, 83–105. Logan: Utah State University Press, 2008.

Mootz Francis J., III. "Vico, Llewellyn, and the Task of Legal Education." *Loyola Law Review* 57 (2011): 135–56.

Morrison, Adele M. "Changing the Domestic Violence (Dis)Course: Moving from White Victim to Multicultural Survivor." *UC Davis Law Review* 39 (2006): 1061–1118.

Mountford, Roxanne. *The Gendered Pulpit: Preaching in American Protestant Spaces.* Carbondale: Southern Illinois University Press, 2003.

Murphy, James J. "Roman Writing Instruction as Described by Quintilian." In *A Short History of Writing Instruction: From Ancient Greece to Contemporary America*, 3rd ed., edited by James J. Murphy, 36–76. New York: Routledge, 2012.

Naffine, Ngaire. *Law and the Sexes: Explorations in Feminist Jurisprudence.* Sydney: Allen & Unwin, 1990.

Nichols, Bill. *Representing Reality: Issues and Concepts in Documentary.* Bloomington: Indiana University Press, 1991.

Pence, Ellen, and Michael Paymar. *Education Groups for Men Who Batter: The Duluth Model.* New York: Springer, 1993.

Perelman, Chaim, and Lucie Olbrechts-Tyteca. *The New Rhetoric: A Treatise on Argumentation.* Translated by John Wilkinson and Purcell Weaver. Notre Dame: University of Notre Dame Press, 1969.

Peters, Jean Koh. "Habit, Story, Delight: Essential Tools for the Public Service Advocate." *Washington University Journal of Law and Policy* 7 (2001): 17–30.

Piomelli, Ascanio. "The Challenge of Democratic Lawyering." *Fordham Law Review* 77 (2009): 1383–1408.

———. "The Democratic Roots of Collaborative Lawyering." *Clinical Law Review* 12 (2006): 541–614.

Pleck, Elizabeth. *Domestic Tyranny: The Making of American Social Policy against Family Violence from Colonial Times to the Present.* 1st Illinois ed. Urbana: University of Illinois Press, 2004.

Ptacek, James. *Battered Women in the Courtroom: The Power of Judicial Responses.* Boston: Northeastern University Press, 1999.

Ratcliffe, Krista. *Anglo-American Feminist Challenges to the Rhetorical Traditions: Virginia Woolf, Mary Daly, Adrienne Rich.* Carbondale: Southern Illinois University Press, 1996.

———. *Rhetorical Listening: Identification, Gender, Whiteness.* Carbondale: Southern Illinois University Press, 2005.

Reddick, Malia, Michael J. Nelson, and Rachel Paine Caufield. "Racial and Gender Diversity on State Courts: An AJS Study." *Judges' Journal* 48, no. 3 (2009): 28–32.

Reed, Alfred Zantzinger. *Training for the Public Profession of the Law: Historical Development and Principal Contemporary Problems of Legal Education in the United States with Some Account of Conditions in England and Canada.* Carnegie Foundation for the Advancement of Teaching. Boston: D. B. Updike, 1921.

Resnik, Judith. "Asking about Gender in Courts." *Signs* 21, no. 4 (1996): 952–90.

Restuccia, Frances L. *Melancholics in Love: Representing Women's Depression and Domestic Abuse.* Lanham, MD: Rowman & Littlefield, 2000.

Reynolds, Nedra. "Composition's Imagined Geographies: The Politics of Space in the Frontier, City, and Cyberspace." *College Composition and Communication* 50, no. 1 (1998): 12–35.

———. "*Ethos* as Location: New Sites for Understanding Discursive Authority." *Rhetoric Review* 11, no. 2 (1993): 325–38.

Ritchie, Joy, and Kate Ronald. "Introduction." In *Available Means: An Anthology of Women's Rhetoric(s)*, edited by Joy Ritchie and Kate Ronald, xv–xxxi. Pittsburgh: University of Pittsburgh Press, 2001.

Rowe, William V. "Legal Clinics and Better Trained Lawyers: A Necessity." *Illinois Law Review* 9 (1917): 591–618.

Royster, Jacqueline Jones. *Traces of a Stream: Literacy and Social Change among African American Women*. Pittsburgh: University of Pittsburgh Press, 2000.

———. "When the First Voice You Hear Is Not Your Own." *College Composition and Communication* 47, no. 1 (1996): 29–40.

Royster, Jacqueline Jones, and Gesa E. Kirsch. *Feminist Rhetorical Practices: New Horizons for Rhetoric, Composition, and Literacy Studies*. Carbondale: Southern Illinois University Press, 2012.

Russell, Brenda. "Effectiveness, Victim Safety, Characteristics, and Enforcement of Protective Orders." *Partner Abuse* 3, no. 4 (2012): 531–52.

Russell, Margaret M. "Entering Great America: Reflections on Race and the Convergence of Progressive Legal Theory and Practice." *Hastings Law Journal* 43 (1992): 749–67.

Sanchez, Raul. *The Function of Theory in Composition Studies*. Albany: State University of New York Press, 2005.

Sarat, Austin. "Lawyers and Clients: Putting Professional Service on the Agenda of Legal Education." *Journal of Legal Education* 41 (1991): 43–53.

Scallen, Eileen A. "Evidence Law as Pragmatic Legal Rhetoric: Reconnecting Legal Scholarship, Teaching and Ethics." *Quinnipiac Law Review* 21 (2003): 813–91.

Schechter, Susan. *Women and Male Violence: The Visions and Struggles of Battered Women*. Boston: South End Press, 1982.

Scheppele, Kim Lane. "Just the Facts, Ma'am: Sexualized Violence, Evidentiary Habits, and the Revision of Truth." *New York Law School Law Review* 37 (1992): 123–72.

Schneider, Elizabeth M. *Battered Women and Feminist Lawmaking*. New Haven: Yale University Press, 2000.

Schrag, Philip G., and Michael Meltsner. *Reflections on Clinical Legal Education*. Boston: Northeastern University Press, 1998.

Schuster, Mary Lay, and Amy D. Propen. *Victim Advocacy in the Courtroom: Persuasive Practices in Domestic Violence and Child Protection Cases*. Boston: Northeastern University Press, 2011.

Schutte, Nicola S., John M. Malouff, and Johnna S. Doyle. "The Relationship between Characteristics of the Victim, Persuasive Techniques of the Batterer, and Returning to a Battering Relationship." *Journal of Social Psychology* 128, no. 5 (1988): 605–10.

Selfe, Cynthia L. "The Movement of Air, the Breath of Meaning: Aurality and Multimodal Composing." *College Composition and Communication* 60, no. 4 (2009): 616–63.

Seligman, Joel. *The High Citadel: The Influence of Harvard Law School*. Boston: Houghton Mifflin, 1978.

Shalleck, Ann. "Constructions of the Client within Legal Education." *Stanford Law Review* 45, no. 6 (1993): 1731–53.

Shipka, Jody. *Toward a Composition Made Whole*. Pittsburgh: Pittsburgh University Press, 2011.

Simon, Barbara Levy. *The Empowerment Tradition in American Social Work: A History*. New York: Columbia University Press, 1994.

Sloane, Thomas O., ed. *Encyclopedia of Rhetoric*. Oxford: Oxford University Press, 2001.

Smart, Carol. *Feminism and the Power of Law*. London: Routledge, 1989.

Smith, Linda F. "Why Clinical Programs Should Embrace Civic Engagement, Service Learning and Community Based Research." *Clinical Law Review* 10 (2004): 723–54.

Smith, Sharon G., Jieru Chen, Kathleen C. Basile, Leah K. Gilbert, Melissa T. Merrick, Nimesh Patel, Margie Walling, and Anurag Jain. *The National Intimate Partner and Sexual Violence Survey (NISVS): 2010–12 State Report.* Atlanta: National Center for Injury Prevention and Control. Centers for Disease Control and Prevention, 2017. https://www.cdc.gov/violenceprevention/pdf/NISVS-StateReportBook.pdf.

Snyder, Marianne. "Emancipatory Knowing: Empowering Nursing Students toward Reflection and Action." *Journal of Nursing Education* 53, no. 2 (2014): 65–69.

Southworth, Ann. "Lawyer-Client Decisionmaking in Civil Rights and Poverty Practice: An Empirical Study of Lawyers' Norms." *Georgetown Journal of Legal Ethics* 9 (1996): 1101–55.

Spivak, Gayatri Chakravorty. "Can the Subaltern Speak?" In *Marxism and the Interpretation of Culture,* edited by Cary Nelson and Lawrence Grossberg, 271–313. Urbana: University of Illinois Press, 1988.

Sprague, Rosamond Kent, ed. *The Older Sophists.* Columbia: University of South Carolina Press, 1972.

Straus, Murray. "Victims and Aggressors in Marital Violence." *American Behavioral Scientist* 23, no. 5 (1980): 681–704.

Sullivan, Dale L. "A Closer Look at Education as Epideictic Rhetoric." *Rhetoric Society Quarterly* 23, no. 3/4 (1994): 70–89.

Sullivan, William M., Anne Colby, Judith Welch Wegner, Lloyd Bond, and Lee S. Shulman. *Educating Lawyers: Preparation for the Profession of Law.* Carnegie Foundation for the Advancement of Teaching. Stanford: Jossey-Bass, 2007.

Toulmin, Stephen E. *The Uses of Argument.* Updated ed. Cambridge: Cambridge University Press, 2003.

US Department of Justice. Office of Justice Programs. Bureau of Justice Statistics. *Intimate Partner Violence, 1993–2010,* by Shannan Catalano. NCJ 239203. November 2012. http://www.bjs.gov/content/pub/pdf/ipv9310.pdf.

Vaughan, Sharon Rice. "The Last Refuge: Shelter for Battered Women." *Victimology: An International Journal* 4 (1979): 113–19.

Vieira, Meredith. "Framingham Eight." *Turning Point.* July 20, 1994. ABC News Classics, 2008. DVD.

Walker, Jeffrey. *The Genuine Teachers of This Art: Rhetorical Education in Antiquity.* Columbia: University of South Carolina Press, 2011.

Walker, Lenore, E. A. *The Battered Woman Syndrome.* 3rd ed. New York: Springer, 2009.

Weiss, Robert S. *Learning from Strangers: The Art and Method of Qualitative Interview Studies.* New York: Free Press, 1994.

Welch, Nancy. *Living Room: Teaching Public Writing in a Privatized World.* Portsmouth, NH: Heinemann, 2008.

Wetlaufer, Gerald D. "Rhetoric and Its Denial in Legal Discourse." *Virginia Law Review* 76, no. 8 (1990): 1545–97.

White, James Boyd. *From Expectation to Experience: Essays on Law and Legal Education.* Ann Arbor: University of Michigan Press, 2000.

———. *Heracles' Bow: Essays on the Rhetoric and Poetics of Law.* Madison: University of Wisconsin Press, 1985.

———. *Justice as Translation: An Essay in Cultural and Legal Criticism.* Chicago: University of Chicago Press, 1990.

White, Lucie E. "Subordination, Rhetorical Survival Skills, and Sunday Shoes: Notes on the Hearing of Mrs. G." *Buffalo Law Review* 38, no. 1 (1990): 1–58.

Williams, Patricia. *The Alchemy of Race and Rights.* Cambridge, MA: Harvard University Press, 1991.

———. *Seeing a Color-Blind Future: The Future of Race.* New York: Noonday Press, 1997.

Zompetti, Joseph P. "The Role of Advocacy in Civil Society." *Argumentation* 20 (2006): 167–83.

Index